Corporate Fraud

Corporate Fraud

Case Studies in Detection and Prevention

JOHN D. O'GARA

WILEY

John Wiley & Sons, Inc.

For general information on our other products and services, or technical support, please contact our Customer Care Department within the United States at 800-762-2974, outside the United States at 317-572-3993 or fax 317-572-4002.

Wiley also publishes its books in a variety of electronic formats. Some content that appears in print may not be available in electronic books.

Printed in the United States of America

ISBN 0-471-49350-3

10 9 8 7 6 5 4 3 2 1

About the Author

John D. (Jack) O'Gara is retired Senior Director—Audit for a Fortune 250 multi-industrial company. O'Gara has managed internal audit departments for three Fortune 250 companies for "multiple decades." Prior to that, he spent six years in Big Eight (at that time) public accounting, including consulting and two years' international residency in Brussels, Belgium, and in Kuwait. He was president of the Central Ohio chapter of the Institute of Internal Auditors (IIA) in 1999–2000, and was the conference chairman for the IIA 2000 Central Regional Conference. He is currently on the IIA Central Ohio chapter board of governors.

O'Gara is currently developing an interactive online case-study-based version of the types of management fraud and corruption depicted in this book and has presented seminars on the topic of management fraud. He says that a fraud investigation while he was in public accounting sparked his interest in management fraud; it has been his avocation as well as his vocation ever since. As such, he has maintained continuing correspondence with major fraud practitioners for the last 20 years and has drawn from that correspondence in presenting certain cases herein.

About the Institute
of Internal Auditors

The Institute of Internal Auditors (IIA) is the primary international professional association, organized on a worldwide basis, dedicated to the promotion and development of the practice of internal auditing. The IIA is the recognized authority, chief educator, and acknowledged leader in standards, education, certification, and research for the profession worldwide. The Institute provides professional and executive development training, educational products, research studies, and guidance to more than 80,000 members in more than 100 countries. For additional information, visit the Web site at *www.theiia.org*.

Preface

Approximately 80 percent of this book had been drafted prior to Enron exploding on the national consciousness. My initial emphasis was exclusively on major management fraud *against* the organization, which would exclude financial reporting. After Enron, I held up: I thought the interest in management non-financial-statement fraud would be diminished, if not eclipsed. Moreover, I felt that the developing Enron saga might render the collected case studies paltry in comparison.

As the Enron story unfolded, however, it became clear that nothing that I had written needed to change: the Enron case had all of the elements and dynamics discussed herein because it was first an overarching management fraud and only secondly a financial-reporting fraud. On February 11, 2002, the Business Roundtable commented that Enron ". . . appears at this point to derive fundamentally from a massive *breach of trust*" [emphasis ours]— which is what all management fraud ultimately entails.

I had originally intended to omit fraudulent financial reporting, not because it was insignificant, but because so much on the topic was already available in the professional literature. The day after I presented the dynamics of management non-financial-statement fraud to the IIA International Conference, however, the WorldCom "Accounting 101" fraud hit the news and brought home the *interrelationship* of all elements of management fraud. To consider one element of management fraud more important than any other is to miss the point: *Major management fraud is all about leveraging positional power and is an interrelated top-down phenomenon—fraud for the organization leads to fraud against the organization, and vice versa.*

Consequently, senior management financial-reporting fraud *for* and operating-management fraud and corruption *against* the organization are not independent. Moreover, the forensic auditor of the future will identify symptoms of both by way of continuous monitoring using information technology to identify the footprints and early warnings available in the data of the organization. Although operating-management corruption typically occurs off the books, continuous monitoring symptoms will be recognizable in the data available within the organization's records once a market perspective is established.

Thus, I have broadened the focus to include corporate governance and top-level forensic issues, as well as other aspects of fraud *for* the organization. Although this is not about Enron or WorldCom, you will find much about the Enron and WorldCom dynamics reflected in the concepts illustrated by these case studies.

The primary fraud role of the internal audit function is recognition of the symptoms indicating that fraud may have occurred. Since major management fraud involves leveraging positional power more than it involves taking advantage of internal control weaknesses, effective recognition requires a management as well as an accounting perspective. Recognition of major management fraud is an art rather than a science, and it depends on a principle-based understanding of the dynamics.

In keeping with the principle-based aspect of recognition, I have started the sections devoted to the particular fraud classification with a discussion of the concept behind that type of fraud. Then, I present a brief discussion of the principles, followed by a list of specific symptoms and an illustrative case study (or studies).

The case studies are totally fictional. None of them happened as depicted herein, although all *could* have happened as so portrayed. The cases are designed to illustrate the principles and concepts of their respective sections, as well as to entertain. The characters, events, and incidents are drawn from the author's imagination and are not to be construed as real. Any resemblance to actual events or persons, living or dead, is entirely coincidental.

Contents

Corporate Fraud

Overview

VARIETIES OF FRAUD/PERSPECTIVE

The contention of this book is that major management fraud is primarily a zero-sum game: fraud against the organization, for the benefit of the individual ("I win, you lose"), with the largest single area of loss resulting from conflict-of-interest corruption. To start, we will examine the landscape and define the terminology.

> Fraud encompasses an array of irregularities and illegal acts characterized by intentional deception. It can be perpetrated for the benefit of or to the detriment of the organization and by persons outside as well as inside the organization.[1]

The primary emphasis in this book is on major fraud perpetrated to the detriment of (*against*) the organization for personal gain by individuals occupying positions of trust and influence in management positions (inside). The secondary emphasis is on management fraud for the benefit of (*for*) the organization, with a focus on the interrelationship between fraud *for* and *against* the organization. It goes without saying that fraud for the organization invariably involves some personal benefit for the perpetrator.

In discussing fraud, I am reminded of the tale of the six blind men describing an elephant, in which the first blind man describes it in terms of its trunk, the second in terms of its ears, and so on. The point is that fraud assumes various guises, and your perspective will shape your perception of what typically constitutes fraud.

Actually, the fraud elephant has at least two dimensions. The first dimension is the *type of fraud:*

- Internal misappropriation or corruption (fraud *against* the organization)
- Fraudulent financial reporting (fraud *for* the organization)
- Other fraud for the organization (various forms of bribery and corruption, money laundering, etc.)
- External fraud against the organization (e.g., credit card fraud)

This book examines the first three types of fraud, with the primary emphasis on the first one.

The second dimension is the *class of perpetrator:*

- Management
- Employee
- Nonemployee

Again, this book emphasizes the first class. Since an essential ingredient in fraud is the ability of the perpetrator to exercise significant control, these types of fraud could also potentially involve nonmanagement individuals who could exert such influence over extended periods of time.

The organizational business environment and context could be considered a third dimension of fraud. Fraud is shaped by the organization in which it occurs. The form that the fraud takes depends on whether the organization is governmental, not-for-profit, manufacturing, financial service, retail, or of some other nature.

In 2002, the Association of Certified Fraud Examiners (ACFE) issued an update to its landmark 1996 "Report to the Nation on Occupational Fraud and Abuse." The 2002 report asserted that 16 percent of all frauds involved losses of $1 million or more. Since the ACFE data indicate that 5 percent of all fraud is financial-reporting fraud, which typically exceeds $1 million, at least 11 percent of all fraud would be million-dollar fraud that *does not* involve financial reporting.[2] This 11 percent constitutes the primary focus in this book: major management fraud *against* the organization.

Here are some additional factors derived from the ACFE "Reports to the Nation"[3]:

- Excluding financial reporting, the median loss in each management-committed fraud is five times higher than that in each employee-committed fraud (see Appendix C).

- The median loss from each instance of corruption ($530,000) is 6.6 times that from asset misappropriation ($80,000).

Given these statistics, the logical conclusion is that a considerable majority of serious fraud against organizations involves management and entails corruption rather than misappropriation.

In the interest of verbal shorthand, this book frequently refers to fraud against the organization as *management fraud* (or, in the case of bribery and corruption against the organization, *operating-management fraud*) rather than "management non-financial-statement fraud against the organization," which would be technically more correct. Please see Chapter 2 for further development of the perspective based on the ACFE data.

Considerably oversimplified, major instances of fraud tend to follow a pattern that corresponds to the positional authority of the particular management group: Fraudulent financial reporting typically is at the direction of senior management, major instances of fraud involving corruption and conflict of interest are at the direction of operating management, and major asset-misappropriation schemes are typically orchestrated by administrative management.

By the way, the particular perspective presented in this book derives from the author's experience in managing internal audit functions for 31 years for Fortune 250 industrial companies. The case studies that illustrate principles of management fraud against the organization throughout this book are drawn from that point of view. My elephant will probably be somewhat different from yours on the surface; however, the underlying principles and dynamics should be the same.

This book takes the following points of view:

- The dynamics of management fraud are different from those of employee accounting-cycle fraud—for example, management fraud against the organization is frequently relational; employee accounting-cycle fraud is transactional (see "Characteristics" in Chapter 3).

- As noted earlier, management fraud involves using positional power rather than taking advantage of internal control weaknesses.

- Financial-reporting fraud occurs at the top of the organization and is committed by senior management; management non-financial-statement fraud against the organization is usually committed by nonexecutive management.

- Operating management will typically commit bribery and corruption types of fraud, whereas administrative managers are more apt to commit asset-misappropriation types of fraud (see "Classifications" in Chapter 2, and "Financial Reporting" in Chapter 7).

- Typically, operating-management bribery and corruption fraud, the greatest single area of loss from occupational fraud, is "off the books"; administrative-management asset-misappropriation fraud is "on the books."

- Financial-reporting and operating-management frauds are interrelated—fraud *for* the organization usually leads to fraud *against* the organization (see "Bullet-Proof and Invisible Leads to Flaunting" in Chapter 4).

- While not estimable with precision, data from the ACFE indicate that management corruption (i.e., non-financial-statement fraud) represents the largest single area of loss from occupational fraud (see "1996 and 2002 Association of Certified Fraud Examiners Reports to the Nation" in Chapter 2 and Appendix D).

- Management non-financial-statement fraud has not received proportionate recognition in the professional literature, particularly given that it represents the largest single category of loss from occupational fraud (see "More Than Fraudulent Financial Statements" later in this chapter).

- Effective prevention depends on the probability of detection and prosecution more than on any other single factor, because management fraud typically involves override rather than taking advantage of control weaknesses (see Chapter 10 in particular, but this is a recurring theme throughout this book).

- Management non-financial-statement fraud has a pronounced risk/reward dynamic: the ability to keep the effect off the income statement, thereby avoiding detection, coupled with a belief that the fraud will not be prosecuted if detected, leads to this type of major fraud (see "Major

Management Fraud Is Different" later in this chapter, "Opportunities Afforded by the System for Performance Accountability" in Chapter 3, and "Bullet-Proof and Invisible Leads to Flaunting" in Chapter 4).

- Recognition and detection of management non-financial-statement fraud require a broad business perspective that extends well beyond traditional accounting (this is a pervasive concept in this book—see "Managerial as Well as Accounting Perspective" in Chapter 10).

- For the preceding and other reasons, management fraud is significantly underdetected. Moreover, when it is recognized, it is all too frequently not prosecuted. The risk/reward implications of underdetection and underprosecution are obvious (see "The Risk/Reward Dynamic" in Chapter 10).

- Due to the greater complexity of management corruption and the broader skill set required to investigate such fraud, the primary responsibility of internal audit personnel is recognition (see "Emphasis: Recognition and Detection—Case Studies" later in this chapter).

- From the standpoint of major loss and the total effect on the organization, management non-financial-statement fraud is the greatest fraud challenge for internal auditors (see "Major Management Fraud Is Different" later in this chapter and the concluding statement in Chapter 10).

The recognition signals—symptoms and red flags—for management fraud in your organization will be different from the red flags for employee fraud. This book provides examples of red flags derived from multiple organizations, but the specific flags for your organization are dependent on your particular culture and business context. Typically, these are organization-specific, and I would encourage you to develop your own.

MORE THAN FRAUDULENT FINANCIAL STATEMENTS

On hearing the phrase "major management fraud," an internal auditor's first thought is usually about fraudulent financial reporting. However, the primary emphasis in this book is on other kinds of management fraud, in part because fraudulent financial reporting is the one area of management fraud that the professional literature has dealt with extensively. More important (and the real reason for this book's focus) is that management non-financial-statement fraud entails significantly more loss than does fraudulent financial reporting.

Total losses from management fraud against organizations are larger than losses due to all other variations of internal fraud. Using admittedly soft numbers—estimates based on estimates—the projected annual loss from management misappropriation and corruption was arguably at least three times that of the annual loss to investors from financial-statement fraud during the six years through 2001.

This book estimates (please see Appendix D) that, normally, slightly more than *60 percent of all loss from occupational fraud is due to management non-financial-statement fraud*—that is, fraud against the organization. Although Enron, WorldCom, and their confreres would impact that ratio, it is safe to say that management non-financial-statement fraud against organizations accounts for a majority of all loss from occupational fraud, at least during more normal times. Consequently, this book deals with fraudulent financials primarily as manifestations of the underlying dynamics of management fraud, particularly the interrelationship between fraud for and fraud against the organization. We approach fraudulent financial reporting from an organizational and managerial perspective—that of corporate governance or the tone at the top—rather than employing a debit-and-credit or internal accounting control focus.

While presenting a much broader emphasis than just that of fraudulent financial reporting, this book limits the attention paid to fraud prevention and deterrence from an internal control perspective, and to specific controls to prevent accounting and basic employee fraud. This is not because these areas are unimportant; obviously, they are. However, these topics are already adequately addressed in the existing professional literature; furthermore, they are less important for the prevention of operating and senior management fraud, which involves the positional override of established controls.

EMPHASIS: RECOGNITION AND DETECTION—CASE STUDIES

The emphasis of this book is on fraud recognition and detection. To that end, it employs a case-study approach that illustrates symptoms of fraud. The primary focus is on the concept underlying the particular type of fraud, and only brief discussion is provided. The intent is not to provide a textbook but rather to illustrate different types of fraud through case studies meant to engage and entertain readers.

Much of the material is addressed to readers on the level of relatively experienced internal auditors or investigators. However, the emphasis on principles and case studies will benefit anyone in an organizational environment who has an interest in recognizing and detecting management fraud—public accountants, chief financial officers (CFOs), audit committees, operating managers, and so on. In addition, the conceptual, principle-based approach should be useful for students just embarking on their professional careers.

All competent professional internal auditors should have the ability to recognize the red flags and symptoms that indicate the possible existence of management fraud, and they should also be able to perform diagnostic procedures to assess the probability of occurrence. Investigation of cases of more complex management fraud beyond determining whether fraud probably occurred normally requires specialized experience and skills. Nevertheless, we cannot overemphasize the importance of recognition. Simply put, recognition must occur before investigation can start.

According to the Institute of Internal Auditors (IIA), "The internal auditor should have sufficient knowledge to identify the indicators of fraud but is not expected to have the expertise of a person whose primary responsibility is detecting and investigating fraud."[4] Furthermore, the IIA maintains that "[d]etection of fraud consists of identifying indicators of fraud sufficient to warrant recommending an investigation."[5]

This book covers the relevant principles such that an experienced internal auditor would be equipped to carry the recognition process through to detection as well as assess the probability of occurrence. Thereafter, certain specialized aspects of forensic investigation are essentially paralegal and technical, and thus are beyond the scope of this text. However, the book offers sufficient guidance for experienced internal auditors to hold up their end while working as part of an investigative team with representatives from the security and law functions.

MAJOR MANAGEMENT FRAUD IS DIFFERENT

Major management fraud differs from the typical employee fraud in its characteristics as well as its frequency. The red flags and symptoms are different, and it is recognized, detected, and investigated in a different manner. Although most fraud is committed by employees (58 percent), management fraud occurs significantly more frequently on a per capita basis, because of the greater opportunity.

There are two important factors that recur in the various case studies presented in this book:

1. Major management fraud against the organization is mostly off the books or, more accurately, off the P&L (profit-and-loss statement). This is a matter of avoidance of detection. For this reason, an understanding of the anticipated operating results from a market-based business rather than an accounting perspective is imperative for recognition and detection.

2. An important dynamic in fraud against the organization is the belief that the fraud would not be prosecuted even if it were detected—as, for example, when the perpetrator "has something" (equally incriminating) on the company or superior.

An example of the first factor is unexpected windfall profits that can be diverted in off-the-books fraud or used to absorb excessive charges related to fraud on the books. This practice permits undetected fraud for extended periods. Chapter 3 expands on the practice of obscuring the P&L in the section entitled "Opportunities Afforded by the System for Performance Accountability."

The second factor—a belief by the perpetrator of the fraud that even if the fraud were detected it would not be prosecuted—is related to the idea that fraud *for* the organization leads to fraud *against* the organization, and vice versa. This conviction on the part of the perpetrator can derive from having some incriminating information on the company or superior or it might simply be the result of an apparent track record of non prosecution of management fraud that exists at many organizations. Chapter 4 discusses this further in the section entitled "Bullet-Proof and Invisible Leads to Flaunting."

The ACFE estimates that the average company loses as much as 6 percent of its gross revenue to all forms of occupational fraud and abuse.[6] Although the true total is most likely considerably lower—say, 1.5 to 2 percent—even that economic cost is staggering. A more subtle cost is the organizational emotional trauma related to betrayal by trusted employees.

Major management fraud against organizations is particularly difficult for most internal audit departments to detect because effective recognition requires a broader perspective than just that of traditional accounting. This major management fraud is the greatest fraud challenge for internal auditors because the total losses are more significant than with other types of fraud, and the organizational trauma and loss of business are more severe. Moreover, because the fraud is frequently off the books and usually more complex, it is the most difficult to detect and investigate successfully.

CHAPTER 2

Perspective (ACFE Studies)

Much has been (and continues to be) written about fraud from the perspective of fraudulent financial reporting or employee accounting-cycle fraud. While these are valuable frames of reference for internal audit fraud detection, they do not capture the largest single area of fraud loss: major frauds perpetrated from inside the organization for personal gain by individuals occupying positions of trust and influence in management.

1996 AND 2002 ACFE REPORTS TO THE NATION

In 1996, the ACFE published a report on fraud and white-collar crime in the United States: the "Report to the Nation on Occupational Fraud and Abuse". This report and the related book, *Occupational Fraud and Abuse,*[1] form the starting point for much of the analysis and the classification system presented here.

In the spring of 2002, the ACFE published an update indicating that, basically, nothing has changed other than a slight alteration in the relative percentages between the three major categories. The percentages and amounts of employee- and management-committed fraud remained the same. Because more data are available for the 1996 report (largely in *Occupational Fraud and Abuse*), most of the detailed analyses in this book are based on that one rather than the update.

The 1996 "Report to the Nation" divided occupational fraud into three broad categories: asset misappropriations (approximately 80 percent of the instances reported), bribery and corruption (about 15 percent), and fraudulent financial statements (about 5 percent).[2] In the 2002 report, the same categories broke down as 5 percent, 13 percent, and 86 percent, respectively (exceeding 100 percent in total because some cases involved more than one type of fraud; see Exhibit 2.1).[3]

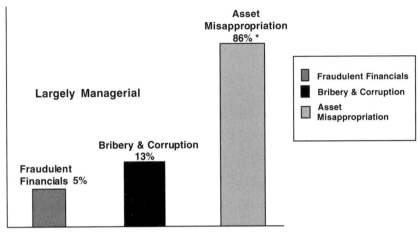

* Exceeds 100% because some cases involved more than one type of fraud

EXHIBIT 2.1 **Fraud against the Organization: Frequency by Broad Categories (ACFE 2002 Report)**

Fraudulent financial statements and bribery and corruption are predominantly managerial fraud; fraudulent financials are almost entirely the province of executive management, while corruption is largely an offense of operating management. Larger asset misappropriations are typically committed by administrative managers; however, on the basis of frequency, employees dominate this category. (The author's estimate is that the total loss from asset misappropriation would be split roughly 40/60 between employee and management fraud, with management receiving the larger piece of the pie.)

Interestingly enough, *Occupational Fraud and Abuse* indicates that the total loss as the result of bribery and corruption was slightly larger (52 percent versus 48 percent) than that from asset misappropriation, even though their relative frequency was 1 to 5.3.[4] This indicates the markedly higher loss per incidence associated with managerial corruption.

The 1996 "Report to the Nation" indicated that executives or owners committed 12 percent of the fraud, managers 30 percent, and employees 58 percent.[5] The 2002 report did not break out executives/owners separately, but a chart depicting fraud "including collusion" indicated that the percentages remained the same as the 1996 report: managers 42 percent and employees 58 percent. (This chart actually shows "Employee & Manager" as

6 percent and "Manager or Executive only" as 35.9 percent, which equates to 42 percent.[6] Employee facilitation is simply the typical fashion by which management fraud occurs—rank does have its privilege.) See Exhibit 2.2. Since there are considerably more employees than managers in the workforce, Exhibit 2.2 indicates a much higher incidence of managerial fraud on a per capita basis, reflecting the greater positional opportunity.

The 1996 "Report to the Nation" reported the median loss from executive or owner fraud as $1 million,—$250,000 from manager-committed fraud, and $60,000 from employee fraud.[7] The losses reported from managerial and employee fraud are the same in the 2002 report, and the median loss of the new category, Manager & Employee(s), is $500,000. (Executives and owners are no longer separately identified as a category. One chart shows employee fraud as $70,000; however, employee-only fraud, as distinct from employees "colluding" with management, remains at $60,000).[8] See Exhibit 2.3.

Exhibit 2.3 indicates much greater losses resulting from management fraud, presumably through the greater positional leverage. A particularly interesting statistic in the 2002 report is the assertion that 16 percent of all cases involved losses of $1 million or more.[9] Assume that of the 5 percent of all instances of fraud involving fraudulent financials, each would entail a loss

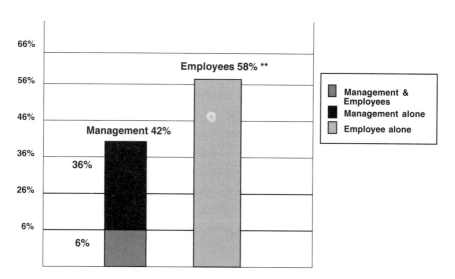

EXHIBIT **2.2**   **Fraud against the Organization (ACFE 2002 Report)**

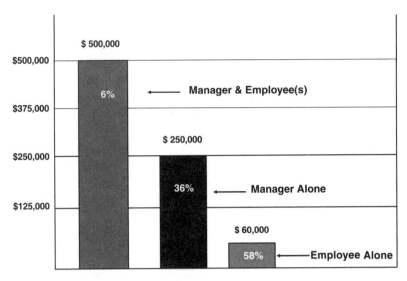

EXHIBIT 2.3   Median Loss from Fraud, by Employee Group (ACFE 2002 Report)

in excess of $1 million. This means that at least 11 percent of all fraud is non-financial-statement fraud entailing a loss of $1 million or more.

Given the relative size of the losses depicted in Exhibit 2.3, a considerable majority of the cases of million-dollar fraud against organizations would be managerial fraud. Further, given the much higher average loss resulting from bribery and corruption, a majority of these cases would be expected to fall into that category. Thus, it is reasonable to conclude that the largest single area of loss would be managerial corruption—frequently referred to as the "sweet spot."

For the purpose of analyzing management fraud, this book considers executives/owners and managers together. As noted, most fraudulent financial reporting is perpetrated by executives and owners. Once we eliminate fraudulent financial reporting, a considerable majority of what is left is fraud perpetrated by middle (i.e., nonexecutive) management. Management fraud against an organization is most commonly perpetrated by this middle-management stratum, and the greatest loss per incidence results from operating-management corruption. Refer to Chapter 5 for a discussion and examples of fraud's sweet spot: corruption—mainly conflict of interest—on the part of operating management.

In addition to the ACFE's "Reports to the Nation," KPMG surveyed 5,000 U.S. publicly held companies, government organizations, and not-for-profit entities in 1998 and issued a report on organizational fraud in 1999.[10] See Appendix E for the results of that study.

The overall data presented by these three reports are comparable and consistent. The relative frequencies reported by KPMG for false financial statement fraud (5 percent), bribery and corruption (15 percent), and asset misappropriations (80 percent)[11] are exactly in line with the frequencies for those categories reported in the ACFE's 1996 "Report to the Nation."[12]

BREAKDOWN OF ESTIMATED TOTAL OCCUPATIONAL FRAUD LOSS BY MAJOR CATEGORY

It is important to emphasize at the start that nobody really knows what the total cost of occupational fraud is. Recognizing that, please see Appendixes C and D for derivations, starting with the data from the ACFE's 1996 and 2002 reports.

One statistic that has taken on a life of its own is the estimate by the ACFE that the average company loses 6 percent of its revenue to occupational fraud and abuse.[13] To the surprise of some members of the audience, a speaker at the IIA 2002 Fraud Conference in Boston (who was not an ACFE representative) suggested that this percentage was based on empirical data from the "Reports to the Nation." This is not quite accurate. Rather, the ACFE came up with 6 percent simply by taking the median estimate of their membership survey responses—nothing more than that. It is at least theoretically possible that this estimate could be correct, but it is more likely that it is considerably overstated. This figure[14] means that an estimate of the total *annual* loss from financial-statement fraud would be approximately *$390 billion.* Clearly, this would be excessive during any normal time.

Former SEC chief accountant Lynn Turner has estimated the total loss to investors from fraudulent financial reporting as $100 billion for the six-year period from 1996 through 2001. This book uses an order-of-magnitude estimate of $30 billion as a "normalized" estimate of the annual loss to investors from fraudulent financials.

Using figures from the 1996 ACFE report to derive the relative proportions of total non-financial-statement fraud loss resulting from management- as opposed to employee-committed fraud (see Appendix C), we would expect management fraud to account for *at least 75* percent of non-financial-statement occupational fraud loss. Using that estimate along with others, we can derive a guesstimate that *at least 60 percent of all occupational fraud loss is due to management fraud against the organization* (see Appendix D). Keep in mind that this is not a precise estimate; however, it is clear that a majority of the total annual loss attributable to occupational fraud is the result of management fraud against organizations. See Exhibit 2.4.

The guesstimate in Exhibit 2.4 is based on hypothetical (and conservative) estimates of the total loss from occupational fraud of 1.5 percent of all revenue ($150 billion), the annual loss from fraudulent financials of $30 billion (see Appendix D), and 75 percent for the loss from management versus employee non-financial-statement fraud (see Appendix C). Please note that less-conservative estimates would simply increase the amount and relative percentage of the loss resulting from management fraud against the organization.

The ratio of the losses from bribery and corruption versus those from asset misappropriations shown in Exhibit 2.4 is 1.08.[15] This exhibit guesstimates the splits between employee and management fraud for bribery and

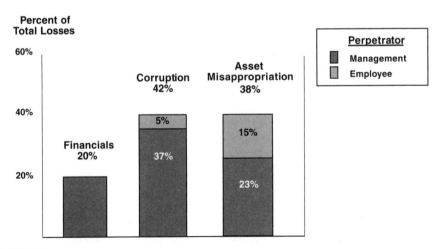

EXHIBIT **2.4** **Guesstimate: Breakdown of Occupational Fraud by Major Category and Employee Classification**

corruption versus asset misappropriation based on the inherent nature of these major fraud categories.

The point of this exercise is to demonstrate the sweet spot of occupational fraud: management corruption (primarily conflict of interest), which results in the largest single category of fraud loss. As noted, this has not received a proportionate amount of attention in the professional literature. A related, and important, aspect of this is that the typical internal audit department's focus on recognition and detection of the fraud possibilities extends only to financial reporting and asset-misappropriation fraud. Such misplaced focus is analogous to that in the old story about two drunks coming out of an alley. One discovers he has lost a contact lens back in the alley, and begins searching for it under a bright streetlight. His drinking buddy realizes this doesn't make sense, and asks why he is looking there, since the lens was lost back in the alley. The first drunk explains that he is looking where it is well lit because "it would be easier to see here."

Financial-reporting fraud and employee misappropriation-type frauds are easier to recognize, but the much more significant losses occur in the shadows of management corruption. We need to ensure that we "fish where the fish are"—that is, look for management corruption, particularly conflict of interest. This basically amounts to sound risk management.

CLASSIFICATIONS

The classifications of the 1996 "Report to the Nation"[16] form the starting point for deriving the classifications that this book uses in the remaining chapters. (See Appendix F for a discussion of the categories and classifications.)

This book previously referred to the category of fraud committed *for* the organization. This category is added to the ACFE report classifications to capture the full scope of management fraud, and is represented schematically in Exhibit 2.5. The relationship between the categories used by the book *Occupational Fraud and Abuse* and those the author considers primarily management fraud (or major fraud) are depicted in a mapping table in Appendix F (Exhibit F.2).

An additional dimension has been added to the *Occupational Fraud and Abuse* classifications: corruption, or fraud for the organization. Included in this are the categories of money laundering, bribery and tax avoidance in the international arena ("black sales"), price-fixing, and commercial

AGAINST **Misappropriation** (Administrative Management)	**FOR** **Financial Reporting** (Executive Management)
Vendor Billing Schemes (Shell Companies) Other Disbursements Inventory Certain Diverted Receipts Schemes (Normally Employee Fraud)	Fraudulent Financial Reporting

Corruption (Operating Management)	**Corruption** (Operating Management)
Conflict of Interst Bribery (Bid Rigging)	Illegal Acts (e.g., money laundering) Commercial Bribery Price Fixing/Bid Rigging International Arena

EXHIBIT **2.5   Major Management Fraud**

bribery. As noted earlier, fraudulent reporting is also classified as fraud for the organization.

The next five chapters correspond with these classifications, as follows:

- Chapter 3 deals with general concepts and principles of management fraud against the organization.

- This is followed in Chapter 4 by a discussion of general red flags of management fraud.

- Chapter 5 discusses corruption against the organization—specifically, conflict of interest, which is the most pervasive form of management fraud—the sweet spot of fraud against the organization.

- Chapter 6 covers major asset misappropriations: vendor billings (shell companies), other fraudulent disbursements, inventory and other assets, and cash receipts diversion.

- Chapter 7 provides an overview discussion of fraudulent financial reporting. This chapter also discusses management corruption for the organization, which includes money laundering, fraud in the international arena (black sales and bribery), price-fixing, and commercial bribery.

The book then offers tips for detection and investigation that are drawn from many years of experience (from the author and his correspondents). These are referenced to illustrative case studies (Chapter 8). Chapter 9 discusses certain computer-assisted audit techniques (CAATs) that can be used for continuous monitoring and relates them to the symptoms of management fraud.

In conclusion, Chapter 10 discusses two hypotheses: (1) that major management fraud against the organization is significantly underdetected, and (2) that, when the possibility of such fraud is recognized, it is frequently not carried through to successful prosecution (for various reasons). It also reviews the obvious risk/reward implications.

This book will also show how Sarbanes-Oxley-driven codes of conduct can increase the probability of detection, along with enhanced internal audit efforts using the principles espoused herein, and that the heightened awareness accompanying the Sarbanes-Oxley efforts, including certain required disclosures, is already having a markedly more salutary effect on corporate prosecutorial zeal.

CHAPTER 3

Management Fraud against the Organization (General)

CHARACTERISTICS

As noted earlier, much of what appears in the professional literature focuses on fraudulent financial reporting or employee accounting-cycle types of fraud. The area of major management fraud against the organization (typically, conflict-of-interest corruption) is underreported, perhaps because this is more embarrassing to most corporations.

This book refers to such crime as "management fraud against the organization"; however, since an essential ingredient is the ability to exercise significant control, this type of fraud could also potentially involve nonmanagement individuals who could wield such influence over extended periods of time.

Here are some common characteristics of this type of fraud:

- It involves significantly larger losses: The average management-fraud loss is eight times the average employee-fraud loss.[1] (Excluding financial-statement fraud, this factor drops to five; see Appendix C.)

- It is relational (e.g., operating-management corruption that employs middlemen or related parties to divert profits) rather than transactional (e.g., misappropriated cash receipts).

- The effect of the fraud is frequently not apparent in the recorded results (off the books or P&L anomaly).

- Because this type of fraud is frequently off the books, after the fraud has been investigated, no adjustments to recorded results are necessary. (Accounting-cycle frauds usually require adjustment to recorded

P&L, not because they involve fraudulent financial reporting, but because they require deceptive recording of transactions.)

- The perpetrator typically is higher in the organization (and older)—a long-term, trusted employee.

- Red flags for this kind of fraud are different. For example, the perpetrator typically does not have the overt vices associated with fraud at the lower level and usually has no criminal background.

- Typically, such fraud displays an entrepreneurial use of proceeds; the motivation appears to be more often ego-driven than need-driven.

- Frequently, others will facilitate this fraud—in other words, an accomplice does the bidding of someone in management—without personally benefiting to any significant extent. For this reason, such fraud will be much more complex and difficult to detect and investigate.

- Fortunately, the extent of involvement of those doing the bidding of someone higher up, but not appreciably sharing in the profits, means that there is a larger pool of potential informants (which is how such fraud usually surfaces).

MAJOR SYMPTOMS OF MANAGEMENT FRAUD

Following are some major symptoms of management fraud against the organization (or major fraud over a period of time by nonmanagement individuals when such individuals can exercise considerable control):

- There are anomalies in the P&L accountability ("black holes") that permit the hiding of the telltale debit or windfall profits that may be diverted (off the books) but still leave an adequate reported profit. (See the case studies "He Was Just Like You and Me" and "Gouging the Customers" in Chapter 5.)

- The organization is decentralized, with local management having control over accounting as well as operations. Frequently, a far-flung geographic dispersion accentuates this. (See the case study "The Beach Club" in Chapter 5.)

- Operating management has leverage against the company or the chain of command as the result of having certain information. Corollary:

When there is fraud at the top, look for additional fraud further down the food chain. (See the following case studies in Chapter 5: "He Was Just Like You and Me," "Gouging the Customers," and "The Beach Club"; and "Tip of the Iceberg" in Chapter 6.)

- There are lifestyle manifestations of the fraud, which are more ego-related—driven by an apparent desire to "be someone" and, frequently, entrepreneurial in nature. This includes engaging in fraud in order to establish a personal business. An additional tipoff might be a major extravagance that is frequently conspicuous, purchased apparently for show. (See the following case studies in Chapter 5: "Gouging the Customers" and "The Beach Club"; and "The Viper" in Chapter 6.)

- In the author's experience, neither management nor significant non-management fraud is driven by that perpetrator's vulnerability resulting from alcohol or drug abuse. However, alcohol or drug abuse and/or "personal problems" on the part of the top manager for the unit, (such as an affair with an office staff member,) serve to disable that individual, thereby creating the opportunity for a significant nonmanagement fraud further down the chain of command. (See the case study "Tip of the Iceberg" in Chapter 6.)

- The organization uses significant middleman companies that are superfluous because they confer no economic benefit to the company and are artificially inserted between the company and its customers or suppliers. (See the case studies "Gouging the Customers" and "The Beach Club" in Chapter 5.)

- Within the organization there is an unwarranted top-down organizational emphasis on only one dimension, which constitutes the organization's overriding objective. One might immediately assume this to mean an excessive emphasis on "making the numbers," but that is not what is intended here. Overemphasis on the bottom line may lead to fraudulent financial reporting, but that's another area. Rather, this overemphasis may open the door to something that can be used to justify unsound economic practices, such as certain conflict-of-interest schemes. (See the case studies "When Incentives Are Too Effective" and "The Overriding Objective" in Chapter 5.)

- Within the organization there is an unbalanced emphasis on the ends justifying the means that includes legalistic workarounds whereby convoluted structures or processes are devised to accomplish business objectives of questionable legality. Notable examples include circumvention of the bribery provisions of the Foreign Corrupt Practices Act (FCPA) and dealings with certain prohibited countries. (See the case study "The TellTale Delivery Receipts" in Chapter 7.)

- The organization has created a discontinuity or vacuum in the control structure, such as taking over the duties of a subordinate, thereby eliminating the supervisory control normally accorded that function. For example, the manager of the local business unit also performs the purchasing function. (See the case study "The Beach Club" in Chapter 5.)

- There are unusual operating conditions or activities for which the established control system was not designed.

- There are inexplicable departures from the usual or established operational or accounting routines, particularly as a result of management override or fiat, and which make no sense unless they are considered in the context of possible fraud. (See the case study "The Beach Club" in Chapter 5.)

- There is an unusually large dollar value of transactions in the affected areas.

- There is an unusually large incidence of cash transactions. (See the case studies "The TellTale Delivery Receipts" and "Steroids for Sales [Money Laundering]" in Chapter 7.)

OPPORTUNITIES AFFORDED BY THE SYSTEM FOR PERFORMANCE ACCOUNTABILITY

The basic concept behind the practices discussed here is the avoidance of the sore thumb of apparent poor profitability that would normally accompany significant profit diversion and/or excess charges. While the focus in this section is management non-financial-statement fraud (fraud *against* the organization), certain dynamics, such as fraudulent capitalization, also relate to fraudulent financial reporting.

From a simplified perspective, the effect of management fraud against the organization can be hidden in one of four ways:

1. The availability of excess or windfall profits, typically unexpected, will present an opportunity for operating management to commit fraud and hide the effect. This can involve diverting profits—for example, using a cutout to capture windfall profits but leaving a modest recorded profit for the company. (See the case study "Gouging the Customers" in Chapter 5.)

    Please note that we are talking about unusual operating conditions that present significant unanticipated excess profits. The key concept is that the excess profits are of such a magnitude that they can be misappropriated and what's left for the company, while modest in relation to the diverted amount, will still appear adequate. This occurs off the books.

    The practice of keeping transactions off the books also can apply to fraudulent financial reporting. In those instances, however, since the motivation is to artificially present a more positive situation, what would typically be moved off the books is liabilities and/or unprofitable arrangements.

2. Alternatively, excess or windfall profits resulting from unusual operational conditions may be on the books and available for offset against the otherwise telltale debits. When this occurs, the fraud is obscured but still on the books. (See the case study "He Was Just Like You and Me" in Chapter 5.)

3. The perpetrator of the fraud is able to "capitalize" the fraudulent debits to keep the charges off the income statement. (See the case study "Tip of the Iceberg" in Chapter 6.) WorldCom was able to use this simple expedient to considerably overstate its operating income for fraudulent financial reporting. A variation on this is the ability to move excess charges through intercompany accounts to pass the performance accountability to other entities. (See the case study "The Beach Club" in Chapter 5.)

4. The fourth variation is the simple use of fraudulent financial reporting to create credits that can cover the effect of the fraud. Frequently, overstated inventory or revenue will be used to create this condition.

The author studied six instances of major management non-financial-statement fraud (see Chapter 4) that occurred in various companies over an extended period. Two involved the diversion of potential excess profits by middleman companies, one entailed the use of windfall profits that were on the books to offset and obscure excess charges, and three involved keeping excess charges off the income statement.

To paraphrase Joseph T. Wells, founder and former chairman of the ACFE, there are no small frauds, only frauds that have not existed long enough to become big. The primary means for a management fraud to exist long enough to become big is to use anomalies in the P&L structure to hide the effect. Please note that this also applies to financial-reporting frauds.

Previously, this book mentioned that an understanding of the anticipated operating results from a market-based business perspective rather than an accounting perspective is imperative. Please refer to the section "Managerial as Well as Accounting Perspective" in Chapter 10 for comments on how one company accomplishes this goal.

How does this focus on operating results relate to potential management financial-reporting fraud? Not surprisingly, the two are interrelated. (The dynamic whereby fraud for the company leads to fraud against the company will be commented on separately.) As reflected in the financial books and records, fraudulent financial reporting operates in reverse from operating-management fraud for revenue-type frauds and parallels management non-financial-statement fraud when it comes to expenses.

For revenue-type frauds (i.e., accounting journal-entry credits), it depends on whether the fraud is *against* the organization (operating-management fraud) or *for* the organization (financial-reporting fraud). The easiest way to commit fraud against the organization is to divert revenue off the books for personal gain. Conversely, in the new millennium, the easiest way to commit fraudulent financial reporting is to accelerate revenue—bringing what properly should not yet be recognized onto the books sooner.

As it relates to the expense side of the ledger, fraudulent financial reporting is similar to management non-financial-reporting fraud in that both have to keep the telltale debits off the P&L. WorldCom's journal entries to capitalize expenses were exactly what a perpetrator of management fraud (albeit an unsophisticated one) would do to keep the telltale debits of fraud from showing up on the P&L.

CHAPTER 4

Red Flags of Management Fraud

SIX MAJOR FRAUD PROFILES— COMMON ELEMENTS

The case profiles that follow occurred in six dissimilar and unrelated companies over an extended period (20+ years); the losses ranged from $900,000 to $3 million (in today's dollars). The author is indebted to correspondents that have provided the firsthand details for four of these fraud case histories.

The first case involves significant long-term leases at short-term rates (for kickbacks), diversion of profits via subcontracting, and substantial bartering (free work for other companies in return for their free work for the local manager). The common elements include the visible use of proceeds (such as the manager's palatial house, valued at more than 10 times his annual salary), substantial windfall profits that were available to absorb the excess charges, and a company with a track record of not prosecuting management fraud. The total loss was $2.4 million (all losses expressed in 2003 dollars).

Another major fraud amounting to $3 million over a six-year period involves diversion of customer payments and issuance of credit memos to cancel receivables. For part of the multiyear period, excess credits were available to hide the effect. Proceeds were used to establish a spousal business; the administrative manager who committed the fraud had leverage against the business unit manager and was able to exercise considerable influence, largely through abdication on the part of the business unit manager.

The next case involves a manufacturing plant that purchased from a middleman company (the local manager) at elevated prices. The loss was $900,000, proceeds were conspicuously displayed, and the company had a track record of not prosecuting management fraud. Excess charges were passed through to affiliated sales companies, thereby circumventing P&L visibility.

In yet another case, export sales were billed to a middleman company, which was covertly owned by the sales manager who had something on the company. Market conditions presented an opportunity for excess return; the middleman captured most of the profits but left an adequate return for the parent company. The proceeds were used to establish the sales manager's own company, upon his accelerated early retirement. The loss was $850,000.

The most complex case was an off-the-books fraud involving a third-party cutout to move inventory offshore. The international spot price was approximately 200 percent of the base cost of material acquired under U.S. supply contracts. The division manager (who had reason to believe he would not be prosecuted) directed excessive quantities to a third-party contract manufacturer as the first step in a series of product transfers and exchanges that moved the material to the international market while disguising the source. The contract manufacturer eventually filed for bankruptcy, resulting in a $2.1 million loss to the company. The division manager profited personally by $4.1 million.

In another fraud amounting to $900,000, a midlevel manager approved bogus charges for payment, and capitalized them as part of capital projects. The payees were fictitious companies (in actuality, the manager); overpayments were also made to real companies that returned the funds to the manager. Proceeds were visible: a very upscale house and car, and the wife's business. This perpetrator's superior in the organization was rendered ineffectual by a messy office affair. Following his divorce 18 months later, the superior, who had left the company, became the informer.

RED FLAGS OF MANAGEMENT FRAUD

The six major fraud profiles detailed in the preceding section had the following significant elements in common:

- *Significant anomalies in performance accountability obscured the P&L effect* in all six instances.

- All of these cases of management fraud involved *an apparent belief that the fraud would not be prosecuted even if it were detected.*

- In all instances, the *personal use of the fraud proceeds was conspicuously visible.* The visibility was less related to a lifestyle of excess consumption than to ego or entrepreneurial manifestations (e.g., establishing a personal business).

- *Significant middlemen or cutouts were present* in all three instances when the perpetrator was the manager of the business unit but in only one of the lower-level fraud instances.

- All of the frauds occurred at *decentralized and autonomous* business units and involved the ability to exercise significant control of the fraudulent activity at the local level.

- The *centralized control system was not designed to effectively handle certain unusual local operating conditions* in five of the cases, and the sixth involved simple override of account coding.

- The *amounts of the individual transactions in the affected areas* were a red flag in five of the instances of fraud.

CONTRAST WITH NONMANAGEMENT FRAUD

You may be surprised at the extent to which the preceding six separate and unrelated instances of fraud shared remarkably similar aspects that were different from the typical red flags cited in the professional literature. Exhibit 4.1 contrasts the red flags of management fraud as discussed here with the "Common Red Flags of Fraud" from the KPMG 1998 fraud study.[1]

You will note that there is a certain parallelism—that is, some dimensions have similar but not identical flags for both management and nonmanagement fraud. Nevertheless, there are sufficient recognizable differences that these red flags of management fraud (or some variation thereof) provide an important additional diagnostic perspective.

The typical red flags of the professional literature are based more on financial-reporting and accounting-cycle fraud than on operating-management fraud. One reason for this is simply that financial-statement fraud has been more extensively studied. Another (and related) reason is that accounting-cycle fraud fits into the established frames of reference of the accounting profession—academia and public accounting.

The more operational and managerial aspects of the bribery-and-corruption frauds do not have such an established professional sphere of

KPMG Fraud Study Red Flags	Red Flags of Management Fraud
Personal financial pressure	
Vices such as substance abuse and gambling	
Real or imagined grievances against the company or management	
Increased stress	
Internal pressure, including management pressure to meet budgets	
Short vacations and unexplained hours	
Extravagant purchases or lifestyle (*some correlation*)	
Ongoing transactions with related parties	Ego- or entrepreneurial-driven use of proceeds
	Significant middlemen—ongoing streams of transactions of major significance
	Having a belief that the fraud would not be prosecuted
	Availability of excess profits and/or "hole" in system for P&L accountability
	Established system not designed for unusual operating conditions
	Magnitude of amounts in affected areas
	Decentralized and autonomous: the ability to exercise significant control at local level

EXHIBIT 4.1 Contrasting Red Flags of Management Fraud

influence to study and promote awareness of them. Moreover, the lack of awareness of operating-management fraud reflects a certain degree of under-detection and underreporting. (See Chapter 10.)

BULLET-PROOF AND INVISIBLE LEADS TO FLAUNTING

On analysis of the six major cases of fraud described earlier in this chapter, the extent to which the proceeds of the cases of fraud were conspicuously visible was surprising. It appears that the perpetrators developed a sense of invincibility—they thought they were "bullet-proof and invisible"—that led them to flaunt the proceeds. The invisibility resulted from the holes in the system of performance accountability that hid the effects of the fraud. The apparent sense of being bullet-proof came from having a belief that the fraud would not be prosecuted even if it were detected. The bases for these beliefs were varied: At two companies, there was a clear pattern of not prosecuting previous transgressors; at two others, the companies were engaged in questionable business practices; and at the remaining two, the perpetrators had something on their superiors.

The two business units that had engaged in questionable practices came to their parent companies by way of acquisitions. These were rogue operations, engaged in questionable practices that the parent companies would not tolerate; however, the same perpetrators of the questionable practices seemed to believe that they could hold the innocent acquiring companies hostage and effectively blackmail them. Fortunately, their assumptions were incorrect.

This illustrates what could be called *entrepreneurial risk:* Privately held smaller companies, particularly those operated by more entrepreneurially inclined executives, have a tendency to play fast and loose. This tendency can translate to fraud in the organization's favor, which eventually leads to fraud against the organization. Because they were able to recognize this tendency, both acquiring companies now perform due-diligence audits employing variations of the red flags of management fraud.

There is one other dimension that provides a useful twist on the standard red flag of vices such as substance abuse and gambling. This dimension consists of having a belief that you would not be prosecuted even if the fraud is detected. In all three instances wherein the perpetrators of the major fraud were not at the top level of local management, they were emboldened by a sense of having some incriminating information on the management level immediately above them. Consequently, here are two useful audit protocols, which are now in effect at the author's company:

1. At a decentralized business unit, when there are indications or a history of questionable or marginal practices that would be embarrassing to the company or when the unit operates in a high-risk environment (e.g., certain international locations or businesses), carefully examine the activities of the business unit from a top-down perspective.

2. When disabling vices or "dirty hands" render the top level of local management ineffectual, carefully examine the activities of their direct reports.

CHAPTER 5

Fraud against the Organization (Corruption)

MIDDLEMEN

Concept

The purpose of a middleman company, as distinct from a simple bogus company for disbursement fraud, is to direct potential profits away from your company or capture excess charges. In that sense, it is an artificial intervention in the commercial stream to obtain a zero-sum profit from your company and/or to serve as a cutout to obscure by way of interposing an entity between the target organization and the fraudulent activity, typically to hide the identity of the counterparty.

Discussion

In the six major cases of fraud that served as the basis for the red flags of management fraud discussed in Chapter 4, three of the four perpetrated by operating (as distinct from administrative) management used middlemen as the primary tactic, and the fourth used a cutout as part of the total fraudulent misappropriations. The fraudulent middlemen companies were created for that sole purpose—that is, they had no other legitimate business purpose. This was one of the key identifiers, although there have been other cases wherein a fraudulent middleman company does conduct some legitimate business in its own right with other economic entities.

In these particular instances, the middleman company was easily identifiable by (1) the volume of business and (2) the recognizably artificial positioning between the normal suppliers or customers and the company. In management fraud, when a middleman company is used to capture an ongoing stream of commercial transactions, it typically is highly visible.

The professional literature focuses on a quite similar red flag. In that case, it is the related party that typically embodies the notion of conflict of interest. In particular, the term "related party" is often used in reference to real estate fraud, frequently in the context of the type of real estate fraud that contributed to the savings and loan (S&L) scandals of the 1980s. In many of those cases, the less-than-arms-length aspect of related-party transactions contributed to the valuation issues of real estate properties. (Please see "Real Estate/Related Parties" later in this chapter for additional discussion on this aspect of management fraud.)

The middleman designation is a subset of the broader term "related party." The ongoing nature of a stream of commercial transactions is the major dimension that distinguishes a middleman relationship from the broader, more generic "related party," which typically is used in the context of a finite set of transactions rather than a stream of transactions.

There is a distinction between the generic and the legal definitions of "related party." Under Securities and Exchange Commission (SEC) regulation S-K, a company is required to report any transaction over $60,000 with a "director or executive officer," which is a very narrow definition. The Financial Accounting Standards Board (FASB) provides a broader, albeit still limited, definition of "related party" in FAS Statement 57: "a member of management," which is then defined as directors, top officers, vice presidents in charge of major business units, and "other persons who perform similar policymaking functions."

Symptoms

Here are some symptoms of fraud involving the use of middlemen:

- Middleman companies that provide little or no "economic value added" benefit. Look at these companies on a timeline basis: When did they appear on the scene? What was the effect on margins? What was the apparent or stated rationale—in the beginning and on a continuing basis?

- Changes in margins not supported by external or inherent economic conditions. See the preceding point regarding timelines and the relation to other things that are happening in the organization at that time.

- Margin analysis—consistently out-of-line margins on sales to one particular company ("sore thumbs").

- A pattern of considerable, recurring shipments to one address billed to other, seemingly unconnected companies.

- Doing business over time with a company whose sole (or at least primary) rationale is to do business with your company. Examine the economic substance of the relationship.

- A pattern indicating a consistent and constant gap when plotting sales prices/purchase prices versus market prices over a period of time on a graph.

- Significant gaps between market or spot prices and contract prices over a period of time for commodity-type materials. Look for sales diversion through cutout companies.

- Inexplicable bankruptcies that leave your company holding the bag or management fraud that is typically inventory-related. In particular, look for acceleration of shipments as the end approaches.

- A variation on the preceding, whereby numerous payments are made to apparently different payees who really are the same business entity, in an attempt to obscure the total payments to the receiving party. An example is payments for consulting or other intangible services.

- A consistent pattern on expense reports of inexplicable entertainment expenses for an individual, with no apparent business purpose. This can be a bright red flag indicating relationship fraud. Look for middleman companies, subcontractors, and the like.

- A variation on the preceding point: a sales manager uncharacteristically handling all matters pertaining to a particular customer, particularly those that would normally be taken care of by the administrative support staff.

- Another variation on the preceding: a high volume of "personal and confidential" mail directed to the local manager, which nobody (including the person's administrative assistant) is permitted to open. If this seems far-fetched, be aware that a Big Four firm lost a negligence suit primarily because it overlooked this specific symptom at a bank that was being defrauded.

- A responsible purchasing individual (e.g., manager, agent, or supervisor) uncharacteristically handling all matters pertaining to a particular vendor or class of vendors, particularly those that would normally be taken care of by the administrative support staff.

- In regulated industries, awarding volumes on a monopoly (i.e., granting all of the business) basis. In regulated industries, the absence of price competition may result in kickbacks as a standard way of obtaining business. Alternatively, the culprit may be a middleman.

- The same monopoly practices employed in certain foreign countries. A monopoly may be the "quid" in a quid pro quo (kickback).

CASE STUDY

THE BEACH CLUB

Background

Audit Manager Mike Williams got a call from his company's manager of supply and distribution (S&D), who was not known for mincing his words. Characteristically, the S&D manager started explicatively and ran on for some time before Mike was able to connect some of the dots. Evidently, there was an inventory shortage at the company's plant in Brazil, coupled with a product quality issue that the sales units throughout Latin America had been experiencing, which the S&D manager felt was somewhat connected.

Because the manufacturing plant in Brazil was on the annual audit plan for that year, the S&D manager asked whether the internal audit team could move it forward and get there soon. Mike obliged and, given the apparent complexity of this project, he arranged to accompany the audit team to the location.

Mike's company produced perfume and marketed it internationally. Approximately 45 percent of their sales were in Latin America; these were supplied from the manufacturing plant located near São Paulo, Brazil, on the coast. The production process involved blending various oils and essences to fairly rigorous specifications. Because of the specialized nature of this process, substantially all of the materials and ingredients had to be imported.

The primary activity of the Brazilian subsidiary was manufacturing, with only limited local sales. The president of the subsidiary was Eduardo Almeida, a rather flamboyant Brazilian.

Investigation

Fairly early in the project, the team's evaluation produced the following facts:

- Mike was surprised to discover that all purchasing was actually being performed by Almeida; the former purchasing agent had been fired two years ago. The explanation offered by Almeida was that he did not see the need for a separate purchasing agent "because I was completely familiar with the market." Mike recognized that this created a void in the customary control structure.

- The purchasing volume analysis that internal audit customarily performed as a diagnostic determined that an unusually high percentage of the purchases (80 percent) had been placed with "Gulf Imports." Almeida said that Gulf provided customs clearance services that the major suppliers did not.

- The plant did the manufacturing for all of the Latin American sales units. The transfer price was at a cost-plus markup, so there was no real incentive for the plant to manage costs.

- The most recent physical inventory showed significant shortages in some critical materials. This was the first time in recent years that the inventory had been counted at one time. In previous years, half the inventory had been counted on one day, and half had been counted on another day a month later "for the scheduling convenience of the public accountants."

- The plant receiving function was under the supervision of Santos Selecao who also maintained the perpetual records.

- As indicated initially, about one year ago, quality issues had begun to be reported by the customers throughout Latin America.

Mike felt that purchasing should receive an in-depth review. Consequently, he called home for reinforcements, and the international purchasing manager was added to the audit team. The quality issues were deemed particularly problematic in that the company sold into a high-

continued

end, upscale market. The S&D manager indicated that continued quality issues could put the company out of business in Latin America.

Mike discovered that Almeida had purchased the local beach club during the past year and regularly held court there. This was a substantial establishment that had been in operation for some years and was apparently quite successful. Mike had actually received the run of the facility the first weekend he was there—all meals and refreshments were on the house for the audit team that day. Almeida was quite open about this business interest and explained that he had come into an inheritance on his wife's side.

Mike also became aware of vague allegations of kickbacks relating to the construction of the plant approximately eight years ago. Interestingly, the local manager at that time was now the manager of supply and distribution, the feisty individual who had requested this audit. More relevant, perhaps, was the track record of Mike's company in not prosecuting management fraud. Mike was aware of two recent instances wherein a middle-management perpetrator of fraud against the company had been allowed to resign without prosecution.

As the investigation proceeded (under the guise of a routine audit), the following additional facts materialized:

- Mike was told that importing and clearance of customs into Brazil could involve significant additional cost. He had been surprised (as well as skeptical) to hear from Almeida that the producer of the major ingredient, who was represented in São Paulo (as Mike determined from the phone book), would not provide this. *The purchasing manager followed up and determined that this supplier actually would provide this as part of the landed cost at no extra charge.*

- The real ownership of Gulf Imports was not quite as easy to track down. The ostensible owners were nominee attorneys. Via follow-up in the local market, it was determined that the apparent owner-operator was an Irish expatriate, Bruce Quirk, a very uncommon name in Brazil. Mike's company's plant accounted for approximately 95 percent of Gulf's business.

Related Party

It appeared obvious to Mike that there was a connection between Gulf Imports and the local manager, Almeida, but how could he prove it? He checked the personnel file and found the answer: The maiden name of Almeida's wife was Quirk; she was an Irish expatriate. *Clearly, Gulf Imports was a "related party."*

The international purchasing manager followed up with the suppliers to compare their price lists with the purchase prices that had been paid to Gulf. He discovered that *the plant had been paying approximately 20 percent more than if they had acquired the products directly.* Interestingly enough, by comparing cylinder numbers of certain products in inventory, the team determined that *these products had been obtained by Gulf from the established supplier* (and it was further determined that the supplier had actually cleared the products through customs and delivered them directly to the plant).

Mike determined that Almeida had actually instituted the practice of split inventory-taking; the public accountants just went along with it. Mike's team discovered that *there was considerable movement of inventory within the warehouse between inventory-taking dates, so much so that discrete accountability was blurred.*

Because Mike was able to discuss soccer intelligently, he was able to establish common ground with Selecao; from that, they moved to the plant receiving practices. Selecao finally explained that Almeida would periodically bring him invoices from Gulf; he was instructed to prepare receiving reports and enter the quantities as having been received. Selecao said that *the particular products for which this had been done were the ones that eventually showed the physical inventory shortages.*

Resolution

As indicated, the quality problems were regarded as particularly troublesome. The international purchasing manager arranged for samples of material from inventory to be sent to a lab for analysis. The results were significant: Substantial amounts of material were not the quality called for in the production specifications and should not have been used in production. After more sampling was undertaken, it was determined that some products had not been obtainable by Gulf from the established producers. *When that was the case, a generic version was obtained (at a much lower price) but billed to Mike's company as if it were the brand-name product.*

The investigation was complete. The team added up the quantifiable damage and discovered that Gulf had been overpaid $900,000 over the

continued

past year and a half. Most of this was simple middleman markups; however, the company had also paid for materials never received (Selecao's receiving reports) and, most alarming, for lower-quality materials. The source of the down payment for the beach club had been identified.

When confronted, Almeida admitted everything. He was dismissed, and a note for restitution was obtained, which required selling the beach club. (Mike made one last trip to enjoy the fine restaurant before leaving Brazil. This time he paid for his meal.)

As a postscript, based on conversations with Almeida, it appeared that he thought he was bullet-proof because of the track record of Mike's company in not prosecuting management fraud. Moreover, because the excess costs were passed to the sales companies, his P&L looked quite healthy (Almeida thought he was invisible). It was for these reasons that Almeida felt free to flaunt his ownership of the beach club.

Mike did not pursue the vague allegations about earlier kickbacks. He did tell the team that, based on subsequent conversations with the supply and distribution manager, Mike thought that the manager's motivation for calling internal audit was that the beach club was "rubbing it in."

CASE STUDY

GOUGING THE CUSTOMERS

Background

A large parent company has a subsidiary, Blue Company, which is a distributor for off-brand personal computers (PCs) into the industrial market. The margins tend to fluctuate somewhat with market conditions and are dependent on supply and demand as well as particular "hot" releases.

Audit Manager Juan Menendes was reviewing the workpapers of an audit of this subsidiary and noticed a peculiarity concerning the sales to the largest customer, the Alpha Company: These margins were approximately half the normal margins. Alpha accounted for approximately 30 percent of Blue Company's sales over the past year.

A Second Distributor

Juan asked Senior Auditor Janet Williams to get a Dun & Bradstreet (D&B) check, and they were both surprised to see that the Alpha Company was owned by the former director of sales of Blue Company, Al Clinton. Not surprisingly, the Alpha Company's business was indicated as also being industrial distribution of off-brand PCs. "What's with this?" said Juan. Since there's normally only enough margin to support one distributor (sometimes barely), the insertion of this company between Blue Company and the ultimate customer did not make sense.

At Juan's direction, Janet went back and analyzed sales to this company for the past three years. She discovered that the pattern of approximately 50 percent of the normal margins was consistent over this period; moreover, Alpha accounted for over 60 percent of the sales for a one-year period during which unusual market conditions had prevailed. The most alarming fact was that, during this particular one-year period, which began three years earlier, Al Clinton was *both* the director of sales and the owner of Alpha.

Look to the Market

Juan again had a suggestion: Compare the posted selling prices to the established market prices during the period, which were available in the monthly industry publications. When she was finished, Janet said, "That's why you make the big bucks, Juan."

The established market prices were actually 20 percent higher than Blue Company's list prices (which were established by Clinton) for the period. After following up with industry sources, Janet determined that supply had been tight during this period—it had been a pronounced seller's market.

Next, Janet went back to the bills of lading for shipping addresses for all shipments billed to the Alpha Company during the one-year period of tight supply. She knew what to expect, and she wasn't surprised: All shipments had actually gone directly to the normal customers. The Alpha Company functioned as a middleman for these sales, and added no economic value.

When she contacted a sample of these customers, she found that they thought they were buying from Blue Company . . . and there was still some lingering resentment because, as one put it, "Your company gouged us—we paid 10 percent more than the already high prevailing prices because we needed the equipment."

The economics were clear: During this halcyon period, Blue Company was getting a margin of only about 8.1 percent on the sales. Alpha Company, however, got approximately 30 percent.

continued

Based on this, Janet visited the office of the sales agent on the East Coast who handled most of these sales. He had no idea that the Alpha Company was involved at that time. (The sales agent did say that since Clinton had left Blue Company, the better customers had been picked off by Clinton's Alpha Company, which sold directly to them.)

By reference to documents on file at the sales agent's office and a comparison with documents in the home office, Janet was able to determine that the higher price charged to customers by the Alpha Company represented the price that the customers thought they had agreed to with Blue Company:

- A price had been arranged with the customer by the sales agent for Blue Company.
- This had been telexed to Al Clinton in the Blue Company home office.
- The home office copy of the telex was subsequently destroyed, however.
- The Alpha Company was billed at a lower price arranged by Al Clinton.

By contacting a sample of customers, Janet determined that the invoice chain was completed by the Alpha Company billing the customer for the originally agreed-upon price. (This was the reason that the customers still thought they had really been dealing with Blue Company.)

Resolution

A quick computation by Janet indicated that Alpha had usurped approximately $1.18 million in profits on the roughly $2.78 million billed to Alpha during the one-year period that Clinton was diverting profits through his middleman company.

After he left the company, Clinton appeared to have been able to obtain preferential treatment, perhaps relying on his charm and prior service with the company. ("Do you really believe that?" asked Juan. "No, but let's focus on the more tangible, readily provable aspects," responded Janet.)

Juan congratulated Janet for her discernment: "Keep this up, and you'll be making the big bucks, also—but I think that very soon Mr. Clinton will not be." Juan was correct on both counts: Clinton was charged and convicted, and Janet was promoted to audit manager. Since the significance of whatever subsequent preferential treatment may have been extended paled in comparison to the fraudulent diversion of profits while he was the director, the audit team just chalked the subsequent treatment up to bad judgment by Clinton's successor.

REAL ESTATE/RELATED PARTIES

Concept

Management fraud in the real estate area revolves around the ambiguity of value and the susceptibility of real estate values to manipulation. Frequently, the transactions are with related parties—that is, they are not arms-length transactions—which compounds the valuation issues.

Historically, real estate has held a prominent place in the annals of U.S. fraud. The massive S&L frauds of the 1980s were based in large part on the manipulation of real estate valuations.

Discussion

The value of a commercial property frequently depends on the use to which it is put. In that regard, management fraud in this area might be considered the equivalent of insider trading: using inside knowledge of plans for the future to take a position. This is comparable to front running in the stock market. (See the case study "Front Running" later in this chapter for an example.)

A more subtle variation on this practice, which capitalizes on the ambiguity of value, is disposing of a valuable property to a related party at considerably less than arms-length value, but at a price that still results in a modest book profit, thereby hiding the opportunity loss. (See the case study "Sale at a Modest Profit" later in this chapter for an example.)

The classic method of real estate fraud is to systematically overstate the value of a property by means of a series of manipulative transactions involving related parties before passing the property to the target. This constitutes *flipping*, a practice used extensively in the 1980s cases of savings and loan fraud. This practice involves insiders engaging in a series of simultaneous purchases and sales at successively higher bases to create a markedly stepped-up basis for a property.

Once an overstated basis has been accomplished, the property is usually pledged as overstated collateral to a lending institution by a shell company established for that purpose. Typically, there is no intention of repaying the loan; rather, when the eventual default on the loan occurs, the lending institution is left holding the bag. Alternatively, once the marked-up basis has been accomplished, the property might be sold (via a related-party transaction) to an unwitting organization. The eventual loser in most of these transactions during the 1980s was the U.S. taxpayer, because most of the losses were insured and covered by the federal government.

Given the widespread notoriety of flipping, auditors are now less likely to encounter blatant instances of this practice; however, subtle variations involving manipulations of valuations and related-party counterparties are still a threat, as are the even more subtle variants already described. As in all fraud, the key is to recognize patterns—in this case, those connected to the counterparties, such as how long they have had title, recurrent counterparties, and actual as distinct from cutout ownership.

Another factor to consider is that real estate had become a "parking place"—a repository for laundered funds. However, new reporting requirements associated with recent legislation against money laundering will presumably diminish this practice.

Symptoms

Here are some symptoms of fraud involving real estate and related-party transactions:

- Involving real estate, a pattern of purchases from titleholders who only recently acquired title.
- A continuing pattern of purchases from the same company(ies).
- In a more subtle variation, a pattern of repetitive transactions with ostensibly different parties that inexplicably share a common attribute such as the same realtor or real estate company.
- A pattern of consistently using the same or relatively few appraisers.

- Involving real estate, a pattern of absence of gain on dispositions—sales at or near book value, particularly if coupled with consistent sales to the same company(ies).

- Excessive incidence of cash transactions, which is a symptom of money laundering. See the new reporting requirements.

- When competitive bids are used, a pattern in which the last bid is the winning bid (and consistently just barely).

- Rapid turnover of property at successively higher prices, resulting in a marked increase in price over a relatively short period of time. This is characteristic of flipping, particularly if related parties are involved in the transactions.

- A combination of a pattern of recent beneficial zoning changes coupled with acquisitions from attorneys serving as nominee owners, same owners, or otherwise suspicious titleholders. Look for possible fraud for the organization (e.g., bribery and corruption).

CASE STUDY

FRONT RUNNING

In the 1980s, before the eventual overbuilding, which led to a glut of gasoline service stations/convenience stores that characterized the 1990s, the race was on to find desirable properties and build service stations. Demographic studies and traffic patterns were all the rage.

The corporate real estate manager of a large oil company devised a surefire strategy to provide for an early retirement. Using his inside knowledge of where the company was looking to expand and the specific properties that were under consideration, his confederates would acquire a property shortly before his company would seek to purchase that property. The profits, while not great on each individual property, provided a spectacular overall return because of the relatively short holding period and the low investment required. This manager's undoing came at the hands of perceptive senior auditor Perry Wright.

Instead of testing isolated transactions derived from a statistical sample, Perry was an early proponent of an approach that, 15 years later,

continued

became known as data analysis. That is, he scanned the entire population looking for meaningful and/or curious patterns.

What caught his eye this time was the simple fact that an extremely high percentage of the acquired real estate properties had been held by the owner for only a short period of time. Based on that, he followed up and determined the next curious part of the pattern: All of the properties had been acquired by corporate entities that had different names but used the same realtor.

He pushed further and discovered that all of the corporate entities had the same incorporating attorney as the nominee owner. From there it was fairly easy for corporate security to determine the true ownership.

Early retirement was the next step—but it was not the comfortable early retirement originally envisioned by the real estate manager.

CASE STUDY

SALE AT A MODEST PROFIT

Some time ago, a major South American country established what were known as *reversionary laws*. These laws were directed against U.S. parent company–owned oil companies, and they provided for all properties to revert to the country at some future date.

Shortly before the reversionary date, an informant called the chief audit executive of a major U.S. subsidiary located in that country. The alleged facts were the following: While the reversionary laws were being proposed but before they had actually been passed, the subsidiary transferred substantial real estate interests to a local company at very favorable bargain prices. The sale actually beat the deadline, but it had left a bad taste in the mouth of the local government.

When the audit executive followed up at corporate headquarters, he discovered that senior management thought that the sale of these properties had been entirely on the up-and-up, mainly because the transactions reflected a reasonable book profit. As it turned out, the corporate headquarters management team had been unaware of opportunity loss: These properties had actually appreciated tenfold, and the modest book profit was but a fraction of the true market value.

Upon further investigation by an audit team and security in the field, the circumstances got markedly worse. It turned out that the acquiring company was a front company. The ultimate owner (two times removed) turned out to be none other than the president of the local subsidiary. The local president expressed his rationale quite plainly: The reversionary law meant that his company would eventually forfeit these properties at book value, so he claimed to be looking out for the subsidiary's interests by arranging for a profit, albeit a small one.

Because of the potential for substantial embarrassment in the host country, the transfer was canceled, and the president fired. The audit executive considered himself lucky that the informant had surfaced because, otherwise, the profitable nature of the transaction would have raised no red flags in the home office.

The company instituted a control measure to prevent bargain sales of real estate in the future. It had been a long-standing practice to require appraisals for purchases of real estate. Going forward, the company required appraisals for sales as well as for purchases of real estate.

BRIBERY—CONTRACTING/ SUBCONTRACTING/LEASES

Concept

Fraud in the awarding of contracts normally involves circumvention of the controls designed into competitive bidding by those responsible for administering the process. It is typically an inside job, usually involving commercial bribes. The concept behind such fraud is that the competitive bid process will be overridden or the contract that is bid will not be the one that is performed.

Contracting fraud can also be accomplished by collusion on the part of the bidders, in which case, it basically constitutes price-fixing and is considered fraud for the organizations perpetrating it rather than a conflict-of-interest internal fraud against the organization under attack.

Management fraud in the area of contracting may also involve using the positional leverage for conflict-of-interest diversion of particularly profitable work to other parties, to the detriment of the organization, or considerable use of company resources for personal benefit.

The classic fraud in equipment leasing involves charging a short-term (i.e., higher) rate for equipment that will be kept for longer periods. Variations involve conflict-of-interest manipulation of credits that should be available when exercising purchase options.

Discussion

The simplest method of conflict of interest in contract fraud against the organization involves breach of confidentiality, such as disclosing the amounts bid by other competitors or revealing who the other competitors are. In an even more basic form, it involves awarding a contract with an egregiously excessive profit margin or permitting the substitution of lower-quality materials or performance of less work than agreed to. This is usually accomplished by commercial bribery of the individual(s) awarding or overseeing the contract.

More sophisticated methods basically involve circumventing the control at the point of award by changing the work to be performed after the contract has been awarded, either through a series of change orders or by employing the technique of *unbalanced bidding*. Another variation is simply to overpay the contractor for physical goods that are not readily measurable (or visible), such as underground tanks in service station construction, cubic yards of dirt (fill or removal), specialty structural steel, or layers of paint. A variation on this involves what is called an *AFE rollover:* accumulating costs under an authorization for expenditure (AFE) up to the authorized amount and then rolling over subsequent charges, representing budget overruns, to open but unrelated AFEs to hide the overruns.

Change orders can be employed to authorize substantial amounts of work after the initial contract has been awarded. Since this work is not subject to competitive bidding, the profit margin for the contractor can be considerably higher. Another simple variation is to award a fixed-price contract or lump-sum contract, and then issue change orders for work that is actually in the original scope of the contract.

A somewhat more sophisticated method is to use unbalanced bids. In this case, the bidder is free to "lowball" certain work items, knowing that part of the job will not have to be performed. The elements of work that actually will be performed will carry high profit margins, while the lowball items qualify the bid as the lowest bid.

Here is a simplified example:

Bidder	Bid Item 1		Bid Item 2		Bid Item 3		Total Bid Cost
	Unit	Quantity	Unit	Quantity	Unit	Quantity	
A	$3.00	1000	2.00	2000	1.00	4000	$11,500
B	5.00	1000	1.00	2000	.75	4000	10,000
C	2.50	1000	1.50	2000	1.50	4000	11,500
D	2.25	1000	1.25	2000	1.75	4000	11,750

In this example, bidder B narrowly won the bid. Now, suppose the actual work performed changes to the following configuration:

Bidder	Item 1		Item 2		Item 3		Total Cost
	Unit	Quantity	Unit	Quantity	Unit	Quantity	
A	$3.00	4000	2.00	1500	1.00	2000	$17,000
B	5.00	4000	1.00	1500	.75	2000	23,000
C	2.50	4000	1.50	1500	1.50	2000	15,250
D	2.25	4000	1.25	1500	1.75	2000	14,375

In this configuration of bid items, bidder B is actually the most expensive. However, because bidder B knew in advance that the job that was bid was not going to be the job that was actually performed, B was able to achieve substantial windfall profits.

As noted, management fraud in the area of contracting may also involve diversion of particularly profitable work to other parties, to the detriment of the organization. This typically occurs by subcontracting (see the case study "Out of the Woodwork" later in this chapter for an example). An additional example of management fraud is considerable use of company resources for personal benefit.

Other examples of management fraud in the contract area are more applicable to a treatise on fraud against the organization from external sources and would include devices such as overcharges, particularly against the government, by way of *cross-billing*—charging labor and materials to a different contract from the one on which the costs were actually incurred, typically to shift from a lump-sum to a reimbursable contract. Equipment leasing is included in this section because it frequently occurs in conjunction with contracting (and may be a means to accomplish overcharging a contract), although technically it is somewhat different.

As noted, the basic method of accomplishing fraud in equipment leasing involves charging a short-term (i.e., higher) rate for equipment that actually will be kept for much longer periods, resulting in a considerable overcharge. Variations involve conflict-of-interest manipulation of credits that should be available for prior lease payments when exercising purchase options.

Symptoms

Here are some symptoms of fraud in the awarding of contracts:

- A pattern of subcontracts: taking turns as the bid winner (the same companies work together over extended periods with rotational winners). Look to the underlying economics of the profit splits of the subcontracts.

- An absence of competitive bids, or a pattern of the last bid being the winner.

- A recurring pattern of numerous construction contract change orders that substantially increase the cost of lump-sum contracts, particularly when the change orders do not provide estimated costs. This circumvents the controls inherent in the bid award process and may indicate management fraud.

- A recurring pattern of numerous substantial changes to major construction contract work elements such that the initially lowest (but unbalanced) bids would not have been the lowest if the job that was eventually performed had been competitively bid in that configuration. This can circumvent the up-front controls of competitive bidding.

- Doing business over time with a company whose sole (or at least primary) rationale is to do business with your company. Look to the economic substance of the relationship.

- A pattern of substantial payments to one company for essentially unverifiable services, particularly when these payments reflect substantial budget overruns. Examples of such services include fill dirt, underground tanks, painting services, and material used in erecting structures.

- Substantial overruns in areas that are not susceptible to physical verification (underground tanks, dirt for fill, etc.), particularly when coupled with AFE switching or rollovers to hide the extent of the overruns—a shell company and purchasing or contracting fraud.

- A variation on the preceding symptom, whereby numerous payments are made to apparently different payees, who really are the same business entity, in an attempt to obscure the total payments to that payee. Examples are payments for consulting or other intangible services.

- Inappropriate charges to balance sheet accounts, particularly for construction in progress (and most notably maintenance-type charges). This may represent circumvention of P&L scrutiny.

- The existence of significantly uneconomical leases rather than buying equipment, particularly when this extends over a considerable period of time. Look for a related party (or kickbacks).

- Leases at short-term (higher) rates continuing for longer terms.

- A monopoly—structuring an arrangement so that there's only one provider.

- A responsible purchasing individual (e.g., manager, agent, or supervisor) who uncharacteristically handles all matters pertaining to a particular vendor or class of vendors, especially those that would normally be taken care of by the administrative support staff.

- Uncharacteristic treatment of one company—for example, early payment to one vendor when all others are paid in 45 days.

- Instead of preparing one invoice for X amount, two (or more) invoices will be prepared for X/2 to circumvent approval requirements.

- Another variation on the preceding symptom: splitting contracts to circumvent competitive bidding requirements.

CASE STUDY

HE WAS JUST LIKE YOU AND ME

Background

The tranquility of a California spring day was interrupted for Audit Manager Don O'Byrne by a call from his boss, General Auditor Bill Justice. Bill was calling to tell Don that the employee hot line had come up with an item for his attention.

continued

Don's company, Cox Developers, was a major mall developer on a national scale. As such, they were acquiring land and contracting for the construction of numerous new outlets on an almost continuous basis. To accomplish this growth, Cox had formed an alliance with five major contractors who did all of their construction throughout the United States. They had been so successful in their upscale developments that major retailers were virtually standing in line for a place in the upcoming projects.

The particular information in question alleged that considerable free work had been performed by contractors and that free merchandise had been provided by retailers at the personal residence of Fred Zeigler, the manager for real estate and construction. Although the details were fairly sketchy and the caller was anonymous, Don and Bill thought there was enough information to warrant follow-up. After discussing what was known, Don put together a game plan to follow up on the allegation under the guise of a routine audit, since this particular function was due for review that year.

Don realized that the volume of construction being undertaken and the success of the malls could provide leverage with the various contractors and the merchandisers such that free work and furnishings might be provided at Zeigler's house. Don also recognized that some people might argue that although the free services and furnishings would not be consistent with the company code of business conduct, the practice actually might not be costing the company anything. Don knew, however, that there is no such thing as a free lunch: Free work would indeed be costing his company somehow.

Investigation—Heavy Equipment Leasing

Don wanted to get the lay of the land. He decided to drive out and look at the personal residence where the work and services were alleged to have been provided. As soon as he saw Zeigler's house, he realized he might be looking at something more than just personal benefits.

The residence was part of a very upscale development, Walden Lake Estates, about 15 miles from the corporate headquarters. Don was astounded to see the size and splendor of the residence because he knew Zeigler's annual base salary was $105,000. The place was later appraised for $1.2 million.

When the audit started, Don asked the division controller about various things, including the lifestyle of the manager in question. The controller mentioned that Zeigler had a somewhat lavish lifestyle but dismissed it by saying that he had married a wealthy wife a couple years ago. He commented, "Prior to that, he was just like you and me."

As an experienced auditor, Don knew that the potential indicators would be the *sudden* appearance of wealth and *how that wealth was manifested.* Don was smart enough not to overreact, but he also knew that there is always a story available to justify a particular lifestyle.

Don realized that the existence of free furnishings would be difficult to track, but he thought the excess cost of the contractors' services might be buried in the construction contracts and thus would be identifiable there. So he reviewed the various contract cost details, looking for time charged to contracts but not actually worked on that contract. This would result in overruns for certain cost elements. Don was surprised to find that all of the jobs were in line with the budgets—there did not appear to be any significant nonjob time buried in the construction contracts.

He had more luck, however, in finding traces and patterns of home furnishings—too much luck, he thought. He had hypothesized that these items would be delivered to his company's local warehouse and accumulated until one of the company trucks could deliver them to the house at Walden Lake. He thought he'd have to look long and hard, over an extended period, to find what he was looking for. Thus, he was considerably surprised to find receiving reports for various sofas, chairs, tables, rugs, and so forth. "What's up," he thought. "Is Zeigler opening an outlet?"

Next, his experienced staff auditor brought something to his attention. The heavy equipment used by the contractors on Cox's construction contracts was actually leased by Cox rather than provided by the contractors. Don thought this was unusual, but the explanation offered was that Cox could leverage their substantial volumes and obtain better rates than the individual contractors.

While the leasing arrangements were surprising, what was really unusual was the duration, the rates, and the percentage of rental payments allowed as a credit toward the eventual purchase when that finally occurred—as it had eventually for almost all of the equipment that had been previously leased.

The equipment was always under a month-to-month lease, at a *short-term rate,* which was typically 50 percent higher than what a long-term rate would have been, but the equipment remained on lease for up to 27 months. The average month-to-month lease ran for 21 months. Don

continued

computed that the uneconomical leases had cost Cox $900,000 over the past two years.

Investigation—Fraudulent Debit Dumping Ground

Don then noticed one other significant peculiarity, which became the key to recognizing what had really happened at Walden Lake Estates. The normal account coding process would have been to distribute the cost of the leased equipment to the construction contracts on which they were used. In this case, however, the 50 percent equipment lease premium was being charged to one particular real estate property.

This property was Cox's operational equivalent of a gold mine. Six years ago, Cox had acquired mineral rights to a property that they planned on using for a mall development, as part of their continuing expansion. Their plans changed, however, when oil was discovered on an adjoining property.

Soon, the royalties made this property a healthy profit center, particularly because there was very little cost to offset the substantial oil revenues. In this case, however, after a robust first three years, the subsequent annual profit had been modest at best. As Don followed the excess equipment lease costs to this property's profit center report over the months, he was struck by the sheer magnitude. Something didn't compute. Consequently, he revised his estimate of the potential scope of the fraud.

Investigation—The Reciprocal Personal Work

Don went back to the warehouse receipts for home furnishings and extended his time period. He added up a rough estimate of the total value of the home furnishings and came up with approximately $440,000 over an 18-month period. This wasn't possible—there just wasn't that much furniture that could be jammed into Zeigler's house, large though it was. He estimated that this was at least four times what would have fit into the house.

Don thought he had the answer, but he wasn't sure why the scenario he envisioned would be happening. He thought the devil would be in the details, as is usually the case. First, he obtained the delivery tickets for the home furnishings that had been hauled out to Walden Lake. He was in luck—the tickets indicated deliveries to four different addresses in Walden Lake, only one of which was Zeigler's. (One other delivery point was on the way to Walden Lake, but only 10 miles out of town.)

When Don's assistant found a suspicious electrician's charge capitalized as part of an improvement to the idle property on which Cox was getting the royalties, the answer was at hand. Don recognized that this charge had nothing to do with that particular property—but it could relate to work at a personal residence. He looked up the electrical supply contractor in the phone book and discovered the owner lived at Walden Lake Estates—at one of the addresses to which the home furnishings had been delivered.

By using the yellow pages, Don soon found the construction equivalent of the butcher, the baker, and the candlestick maker—in this case, an electrician, a masonry contractor, a roofer, and a plumber—and they all lived at Walden Lake Estates (except for the plumber who lived at the address 10 miles out of town on the way to Walden Lake).

The pattern was complete. The various specialty contractors, all of whom personally owned their respective companies, had gotten together. Each had performed his respective specialty for the benefit of all the others. It was their crews that the informant had seen working at Zeigler's house. Zeigler's contribution was the considerable amount of home furnishings that he extorted from Cox's mall clients. And let's not forget the kickbacks for the inflated equipment leases.

Resolution

Don added up the excess charges for inflated equipment leases from the royalty property profit center. The total was $830,000 over an 18-month period. That amount, which provided a steady stream of kickbacks, coupled with the "free" home furnishings, financed the palatial estate at Walden Lake.

There was only one fly in the ointment: the track record of Don's company in (not) prosecuting management fraud. Don was aware of three instances in which a middle-management perpetrator of a fraud against the company had been allowed to resign without prosecution. In light of this, Don was pragmatic. He thought that, although he had sufficient evidence to warrant prosecution, it was not likely.

He was right. Management elected to settle for termination and a relatively modest recovery. Don thought the cup was only half full: Although his company had gotten rid of one management "fraudster," it had sent a message that the next manager caught would probably not be prosecuted. Don thought that merely increased the likelihood of another fraud occurring somewhere in the organization.

OUT OF THE WOODWORK

A few months after the initial review, as Don O'Byrne said, "the allegations came out of the woodwork." Four different anonymous telephone calls were received contending, "You haven't gotten all of it . . . more activities went into financing the house at Walden Lake Estates." As an experienced audit manager, Don realized that this was typical, and, in fact, a couple of the calls appeared to be motivated more by malice than they were based on fact. However, there did appear to be enough smoke to warrant taking another look, although the allegations were not particularly useful in that they were vague. The common theme was conflict of interest, with arrangements that were detrimental to his company.

Consequently, Don ran a disbursement analysis that listed payees in descending order of the total annual payments, over a three-year period. His audit group used this to identify significant payees and to look for what Don called "inflection points" on the timelines: marked changes that could be associated with points in time and reasons. Don also customarily identified all significant payees with whom the company was doing business via D&Bs and other checks.

As is always the case, most changes had valid economic or operational reasons; further, most payees were well known or readily identifiable. After follow-up, however, there remained two anomalies.

The first was an appraisal service. Evidently, two years ago, the employees used for preliminary real estate estimates were fired, and this function was, in essence, outsourced to McGillicuddy Appraisal Services. The curious issue was that the continuing volume would have justified three employees in-house. Moreover, the rates charged by McGillicuddy were so uneconomical that the cost was now twice what it had been when the task was performed in-house. Clearly, it was an uneconomical arrangement, but that's not fraudulent in itself.

Since he had been unable to get a D&B on McGillicuddy Appraisal, Don drove by the business address for that company. He saw an apartment building rather than a business outlet, and recognized the possibility that he had uncovered a related-party arrangement.

Next, Don called the human resources department and checked the application form of the now-former manager for real estate and construction. Bingo! One of the references was a "James McGillicuddy." On further investigation, he determined that James McGillicuddy was the brother-in-law of the former manager.

The second anomaly was a company that had emerged as a subcontractor two and a half years ago for the alliance contractors. One suspicious feature of this was that there was virtually no information available from D&B. The alliance contractors used this subcontractor consistently; moreover, the most profitable segments of their contracts were consistently subcontracted to this company.

Don knew where to go next. He contacted the state agency responsible for incorporation records and found out the identities of the incorporators of this company, which had been in existence for only two and a half years. Sure enough, the former manager for real estate and construction owned 75 percent of this company.

Based on the new information, corporate management reevaluated the initial decision not to prosecute the former manager. The decision, however, remained the same. Again, Don could only shake his head and look forward to the next fraud investigation, realizing that the message had been sent to would-be perpetrators of fraud that, if you are caught, you do not have to worry about prosecution.

CASE STUDY

KNOCK THE CHIP OFF MY SHOULDER

Senior Auditor Casey Young had heard about Project Engineer Gil Dove some time ago. Dove had challenged a relatively inexperienced young auditor on an earlier construction contract audit to "go ahead and try to find the kickbacks I've taken." Throughout the audit, Dove kept up this constant refrain, much to the annoyance of the auditor. The auditor commented that Dove reminded him of a schoolyard bully saying, "Go ahead . . . I dare you to knock the chip off my shoulder."

Casey knew that behavior at either end of the aggression continuum—either overly aggressive or meekly submissive—might be indicative of having something to hide. Consequently, when he started the planning for the audit of a major construction project that had been the responsibility of Dove, he was eager to walk the extra mile.

continued

The audit had been requested by the new vice president of engineering. The reason for the request was that a problematic construction project had a considerable overrun, and the VP was perplexed about what the reason could be. The project had a "not to exceed" initial contract amount, but the total project cost was 85 percent more. What had happened? The VP had been told by Dove that their company had caused the overrun; Dove said the contractor, Trilogy & Son, had performed well under the circumstances and was entitled to full payment.

The VP had his doubts, however. He did not have an engineering background; thus, he asked Audit Manager Morris Wright to look into the project and help him determine what had happened. If this particular project had turned out so badly, what was the trend for similar projects?

Morris assigned Casey to the project. Casey was initially surprised at the magnitude of the cost overrun, particularly because the project had been awarded on a guaranteed maximum of $3,298,000, with any savings to be split fifty-fifty. From that humble beginning, the cost had escalated to $6,101,000.

The first item that piqued Casey's curiosity was the magnitude of the total overrun (85 percent), the ratio of the amount of the overrun to the initial guaranteed maximum. Casey knew enough about unbalanced bids to suspect that something like that had happened here—that the job that was done was not the job that was bid. However, he also knew that, strictly speaking, unbalanced bids wouldn't normally apply to contracts that stipulated guaranteed maximums—they more readily applied to cost-plus or time-and-materials contracts. So what had happened here?

His first surprise was to discover that none of the change orders had estimated costs assigned at the time of issuance to establish accountability. Rather, they had been issued basically on an open-ended basis. Even worse, the indicated scope changes and reasons for the change orders were so vague that accountability could not be established for any corresponding reduction in the guaranteed maximum amount of the contract. Moreover, the change orders had never actually been approved, and the contractor had not accumulated costs by change order.

After reviewing the details of the contract administration, particularly the timing of the change order issuance, neither Casey nor Morris was satisfied—nor, to his credit, was the new VP of engineering. Morris suggested that Casey might want to look at all of Gil Dove's projects over an extended multiyear period, and the VP decided that was in order.

Not surprisingly, a similar pattern emerged, although to a somewhat lesser degree. In all cases, substantial overruns followed Gil around like dirt followed Pigpen. According to Casey, Dove "was jinxed; wherever he turned up, major cost overruns seemed to follow." Casey and Morris realized that a consistent pattern of overruns might be due to other factors than just a bad horoscope.

More telling was the pattern of how the overruns occurred: Change orders accounted for all of them, and the ratio of the change orders to the initial bid award averaged 40 percent over the extended period. Most telling was that for all of the more substantial overruns, the contractor was Trilogy & Son. (In fact, on those few projects administered by Dove where Trilogy was not the contractor, the overruns were minimal.)

Casey examined specific line-item bids and contract costs for certain contracts. He found a consistent pattern whereby the lowest unit cost items in the bid were replaced by change orders early in the project, and much higher unit cost items were added.

He analyzed the competitive bids. In all cases, once the lowest unit cost item was removed from the bid, Trilogy would not have been the lowest bidder (and frequently would have been the highest). Obviously, unbalanced bidding and egregious preferential treatment had occurred.

Realistically, Dove had to have been receiving kickbacks or some other quid pro quo. However, the question became how to prove that. In the era of funds transfers to offshore accounts, good luck.

There *was* an answer, however. The most recent Trilogy contract audit clause was unusually favorable in that it provided the auditors access to all overhead charges allocated to the contract. This relatively unusual clause was not for cost-reimbursability; rather, it was for the purpose of setting the overhead rate, which was a factor in arriving at the "not to exceed" cost amount.

The auditors invoked this clause and mapped the P&L overhead accounts that went into the home office overhead allocation. They hit pay dirt: The account entitled consulting expense was one of the allocated charges. Casey requested the details of this home office general overhead account, and, to his great pleasure, he discovered that Trilogy had variously paid Gil Dove $275,000, $411,000, and $633,000 for consulting services in the past three years.

The audit was over, but the legal battle had just begun (although it wasn't much of a battle). Given the results of Casey's audit, his company prevailed hands-down: Dove made substantial restitution, and over $11 million was recovered from Trilogy. Casey thought to himself, "I guess I knocked that chip off his shoulder."

OUTSOURCING

Concept

The section in Chapter 3 entitled "Major Symptoms of Management Fraud" noted that "an unwarranted top-down organizational emphasis on only one dimension, which constitutes the organization's overriding objective, . . . may open the door to something that can be used to justify unsound economic practices." A pervasive example of this in the 1990s was outsourcing. In the name of reducing an organization's body count, fixed costs, or whatever particular one-dimensional metric was the current focus, much activity was contracted out on an inherently uneconomical basis. Much of this was just poor management, but the practice opened the door—in some cases, widely—to self-enrichment via conflict-of-interest arrangements.

Discussion

A basic audit approach to outsourced activities is to analyze the underlying economics and administration of the arrangement:

- Compare the cost of the outsourced arrangement with that of the former in-house activity.
- If the task in question is a new activity, compare its cost to a normative cost if it were to be performed in-house.
- Compare the actual cost to the amount budgeted.
- What risk of loss was transferred to the provider of the outsourced service?
- Is the arrangement cancelable? If so, what are the penalties?
- How transparent is the arrangement?
- To what degree is the arrangement at arms-length?
- Were competitive bids sought?
- What special qualities or capabilities does the outsource provider bring to the arrangement?
- Does the arrangement have an audit clause?

- Who oversees the arrangement, including approval for payments?
- Is the arrangement generally consistent with other arms-length arrangements (on payment terms, etc.)?
- What is the economic return, and is it consistent with the inherent risk assumed by the outsourced service provider?

Symptoms

Here are some symptoms of fraud that occurs in outsourcing arrangements:

- An arrangement structured so that there's only one possible provider.
- A business activity outsourced to a former employee or a related party at an uneconomical rate.
- The absence of competitive bids.
- Uncharacteristic treatment of one particular company, such as early payment to one vendor when all others are paid in 45 days.
- A bankable arrangement that is not cancelable for many years, requires virtually no initial investment (the assets required may have been transferred at gift prices), and entails virtually no business risk for the outsourced service provider while carrying a guaranteed high return. Examine the underlying relationship.
- A pattern of substantial payments to the outsourced service provider for essentially unverifiable services, particularly when these payments reflect substantial budget overruns.
- A budgetary shell game whereby the cost of a function is fragmented or allocated to various centers in such a way that the total cost is no longer visible.
- A variation on the preceding symptom whereby numerous payments are made to apparently different payees, which are really the same business entity, in an attempt to obscure the total payments to that payee, such as payments for consulting or other intangible services.
- A pattern of substantially uneconomical practices at multiple locations controlled by one manager—for example, substantial excess cash balances at all international locations or freight abuses involving one carrier at multiple locations. The concept to look for is inexplicable

occurrences at multiple locations with a common management denominator.

- Potential management fraud. This can be used to generate slush funds.

CASE STUDY

THE OVERRIDING OBJECTIVE

Background

Brian White, an entry-level staff auditor had impressed Audit Manager Stan Wood with his zeal and enthusiasm. He frequently worked extra hours, and his energetic approach resulted in some solid project findings. Brian had worked his way through college and leveraged that experience to good effect. Stan was initially skeptical, however, when Brian approached him with his most recent hypothesis. Stan suspected that Brian's audit reach still exceeded his grasp.

Brian had remembered something he had heard in the course of his introductory staff training: an unwarranted top-down organizational emphasis on only one dimension, which constitutes the overriding objective, may open the door to something that can be used to justify unsound economic practices. Using his prior work experience as a plant worker in a manufacturing operation, Brian thought he might have come across just that sort of thing during an audit of one of the operating divisions.

This business unit produced a high-priced carbonated soft drink, and the company plants had set up a labor outsourcing arrangement whereby the in-plant bottling operations were conducted by contract labor obtained from a third-party company, Kline Services. As luck would have it, Brian was familiar with the production operation, having worked in a similar environment as an undergraduate. Brian knew that this was a very basic manufacturing process that required limited training and low-level skills. Thus, he was surprised to see what his company was paying Kline for these workers.

Brian's company, JKLM Cola, was being charged $31 per hour for regular time, and twice that for overtime. He remembered his undergraduate years when he was performing similar production work for a third of that. He told Stan, "Heck, I'll quit my audit job and go back to being a plant laborer—that is, if I can work for Kline." His point was that this arrangement was so conspicuously uneconomical that something was probably wrong somewhere.

Stan provided some perspective. About 10 years ago, JKLM Cola had undertaken a company-wide initiative to reduce body count. While this was a desirable initiative in the abstract, the problem that had been recognized at other divisions was the way this objective was achieved.

The audit department had already run into instances in which uneconomical decisions had been made in the name of reducing the body count. Consequently, Brian's observation was not surprising and was initially not considered to be malfeasance, just wasteful.

Analysis

In this case, however, as Stan and Brian began to analyze the situation further, the extent to which the initial arrangement was unfavorable, coupled with how it had been consistently administered to their company's disadvantage, raised the issue of conflict of interest.

The following facts emerged:

- The arrangement had been in place for eight years. The original contract had expired after six years but had been renegotiated and extended. Both contracts were essentially "take or pay": JKLM was obligated to use $7.5 million in contract labor annually for the first six years or pay the difference between $7.5 million and what was actually used.

- Neither contract had been subject to competitive bidding.

- George Kline, the owner of Kline Services, had formerly been a supervisor in human resources for JKLM.

- By contract, JKLM was responsible for all costs (advertising, testing, etc.) of recruiting laborers for Kline Services. Moreover, JKLM provided the office space, utilities, and PC equipment. And George Kline was separately billable to JKLM at an annual salary of $140,000 (not bad, thought Brian, considering the fact that Kline had been making $80,000 annually for JKLM).

- By contract, all increases in the Kline Services base cost of labor (including benefits) passed through to JKLM on a percentage basis. Brian realized that this meant there was no incentive for Kline to keep its base costs in line.

continued

- Through inquiries, Brian determined that Kline Services had no clients other than JKLM.

Brian went out on the plant floor to talk with the laborers. Never bashful, he asked them up front what they were making. As he had suspected, their base rate was around $12.50 per hour. What he hadn't expected was that their benefits were practically nonexistent—they told Brian that they were getting only those benefits that were mandated by state law. For that reason, morale was low, and there was considerable turnover.

Brian and Stan first looked for other favorable treatment extended to Kline Services. They were surprised to find that all secretarial hires in the home office also went through Kline Services.

Here is the way it worked (or so they were informed by the headquarters human resources staff): People applying to JKLM for office administration positions would be referred to Kline Services. If hired, they would be engaged on Kline's payroll and would work in JKLM's offices on a provisional basis for three months. During this period, JKLM would be billed $27.50 per hour for each person hired. Brian determined that the workers were receiving $15.00 per hour, with few or no benefits. After three months, the successful candidates would be hired by JKLM, and Kline would receive a $1,000 "finder's fee." Because there were approximately 1,700 employees at the large headquarters office, this arrangement provided a continuing stream of revenue for Kline.

Resolution

Brian and Stan recognized that the overall arrangement with Kline was so egregiously uneconomical that it couldn't have been entered into in good faith. What would be the next step, however? Not surprisingly, given the one-sided aspect of the arrangement, there was basically no audit clause: JKLM had no contractual right to examine Kline's records.

Next, Stan got a D&B report in an attempt to determine the true ownership of Kline Services. The D&B was not useful: The indicated owners were nominee attorneys. Although Stan had contacted corporate security so they could work their behind-the-scenes information-gathering magic to determine the true ownership of Kline Services, he did not rely on just that.

Stan was resourceful, and Brian was determined. Stan pointed out that the plants had gone to ID-card access in the last year, which extended to the third-party Kline employees. Brian obtained the records of the card-reader-controlled access to the plants and discovered a pattern of consistent overbilling by Kline Services: In the year after the card readers had been installed, Kline billed JKLM for 12 percent more daily laborers than had been registered by the card readers.

Based on this and other irregularities that surfaced after an in-depth review of the billings, Brian and Stan were able to use JKLM's leverage with Kline Services (JKLM was, when all was said and done, the only customer of Kline) to get access to Kline's internal records. This mushroomed into somewhat more than George Kline had expected. Brian was no respecter of boundaries—his motto was "look first and ask for forgiveness later." By means of just such a preemptive examination of the internal records, Brian progressed to the promotional and consulting expenses, where he found what he was looking for: payments to the JKLM VP of human resources and to the director of manufacturing.

Based on finding a paper trail of these payments, the examination of Kline's records expanded yet one more time, to a look at the profit-sharing distributions. From this, Brian was able to eventually uncover the fact that George Kline owned only 20 percent of Kline Services, while the JKLM human resources vice president and the director of manufacturing each owned 40 percent. This was the smoking gun they were looking for.

JKLM prosecuted criminally and was successful. The company was able to obtain over $3 million in restitution. As in all cases of complex management fraud, the key step was in the recognition of the nature and extent of the uneconomical practices.

MANIPULATION OF PERFORMANCE BONUSES/CO-OPTING OTHERS

Concept

As performance goals are aligned with organizational objectives to achieve congruence, performance metrics and other nonfinancial quantitative measurements are increasingly linked to personal pay. Frequently, the individual whose incentive pay is determined by such metrics will be the individual who measures and reports the statistics.

When such an arrangement exists, and when a metric-related activity makes no inherent sense (and, in particular, when the process is manipulated and reporting of the particular performance metrics is distorted), look to the incentive compensation system for an explanation.

The individual who is engaged in conflict of interest in general—and in particular by distorting the reporting of performance metrics—will also frequently be co-opting others within the organization. Such an individual who buys acquiescence typically does so by bestowing favors that can be withheld as readily they are granted. These favors are usually something other than salary increases, which, once granted, become entitlements, and they are apart from the ordinary course of business. Perquisites such as excessive or unusual stock options, trips, or lavish entertaining are examples of such internal bribes. In the case of certain overly accommodating boards of directors, donations to favored charities, consulting contracts, and the like have given at least the appearance of a too-comfortable arrangement.

Discussion

When you encounter obvious favoritism and manipulation of staff, ask yourself why. Manipulating staff by pandering and payoffs might be a symptom of underlying dishonest activity. In such instances, the individuals who abuse their positions of power are buying acquiescence from those who report to them. They are co-opting those who would normally be in a position to recognize and acknowledge distorted reporting of nonfinancial measurements for personal gain. In a very real sense, they are indirectly participating in the process and have been corrupted on a once-removed basis.

Lavish reciprocal entertaining is one method of such co-optation. A common and efficacious method is the granting of stock options disproportionately or to employees whose rank would not ordinarily merit these. Another perquisite is free use of the company aircraft. In general, much conflict-of-interest activity is accompanied by the granting of unwarranted special favors to forestall potential complaints.

Symptoms

Here are some symptoms of fraud that involves co-opting others:

- Lavish reciprocal entertaining—for example, continuing entertainment with no outside party present and no apparent valid business purpose.

- Gratuitous contributions to favorite charities of the individual(s) being co-opted.

- Consulting contracts or other sweetheart deals to buy off employees.

- Stock options granted disproportionately or to employee levels that do not customarily participate in such benefits.

- Favoritism in promotions or assignments. In particular, the practice of rewarding employees with positions and salaries beyond what they could command in the open market may not buy loyalty, but it can purchase a fair amount of subservience.

CASE STUDY

WHEN INCENTIVES ARE TOO EFFECTIVE

Background

In many organizations, performance metrics and other nonfinancial quantitative measurements are increasingly linked to personal pay. The importance of an internal audit team in providing assurance of objectivity in this process is clear.

What happens, however, when the responsible executive engages in significant distortions to the extent that they cross the line from puffery into fraud? While the particular line of demarcation may be somewhat fuzzy, most of us would agree that obtaining significant personal benefit under false pretenses would constitute de facto fraud. Just such an occurrence culminated in an internal fraud investigation focusing on the manufacturing manager of a company we'll call Yankee Manufacturing.

Yankee Manufacturing was headquartered in New England. The company made cardboard containers at five regional plants. The economic success of the company had been directly related to the business cycle: When the overall industrial economy was expanding, profits were good; but when overall economic growth slowed, Yankee's operating results were weak.

In an attempt to counter the boom-bust phenomenon, the chief executive officer (CEO) adopted a "balanced scorecard" three years ago. The key was to establish meaningful operating metrics for all departments that would be aligned with the company's basic operating

continued

principles and objectives. A fundamental premise, of course, was that the measurements would be objective and accurate.

Early Results

At the same time, a new manufacturing manager, Fred Irwin, had been hired from the outside with a mandate to increase the overall operating efficiency and effectiveness of the manufacturing process.

At first, Irwin was welcomed by the manufacturing staff. He was personable, made an excellent first impression, and held himself out as a change agent. His predecessor had been overly focused on the purely technical details of plant operations, particularly maintenance. Consequently, the experienced members of the manufacturing staff, who had realized that the plants could be providing a more valuable resource by expanding the range of production, were ready to move into more value-added plant business solutions.

Soon, however, it was apparent to the manufacturing staff that Irwin's emphasis was on style rather than substance. He never bothered to learn the basic manufacturing process. Worse, he was manipulative and prone to favoritism in his handling of the staff. He was actually caught in numerous outright lies.

Not too surprisingly, staff morale and trust deteriorated, and the turnover rate went up. What *was* surprising, however, was that the perception on the part of the rest of the company about the effectiveness of the plants initially increased dramatically. The reason for this was simple: The experienced staff, who had survived the regime of the predecessor, knew how to provide value-added solutions to their clientele because they had been waiting so long to do just that.

Manipulation/Degradation

Fairly soon, however, Irwin reduced the plant maintenance crew to a low staffing level and cut back severely on basic repairs and maintenance. He continued to extol the manufacturing capabilities and pushed the more glamorous internal manufacturing consulting projects, which produced the "flash and dash" that he liked to report to the CEO and senior management. The reported results continued to look good; management didn't realize that very few projects were actually being completed.

Maintenance managers Mike Able and Don Hill were seriously concerned; they were joined in this by the plant engineer, Frank Justice. Frank had asked for a meeting with Mike and Don after work. "This has gone too far," Frank started off the meeting by saying. "Now the dishonest boob is hiding the fact that we're barely performing any maintenance and repair; our authorized staffing level is way too low and we're not even replacing vacancies as they occur; we've virtually disbanded the maintenance staff—we're not discharging our mission."

Mike and Don agreed. They informed Frank that they had attempted to talk to Irwin on various occasions, but clearly he had his own personal agenda. By comparing notes, they began to see what that agenda was.

First, they realized that Irwin had manipulated the operating metrics to avoid disclosing what an appropriate staffing level would be. He had recommended an authorized complement to the CEO that was approximately 65 percent of the actual external benchmark norm, but he noted that "benchmarking indicates we're right where we should be," when the CEO questioned the level of staffing.

More important, Frank told the others that he had been instructed to report a certain percentage of the cost of routine maintenance and repairs as "construction in progress." Next, the group realized that the value-added manufacturing process improvements had also become distorted. To obtain usable performance metrics, the savings resulting from process changes were to be measured and reported. Irwin had overemphasized and exaggerated the estimated dollar savings resulting from these changes, however, going so far as to report totally fictitious projects.

Moreover, he had begun weeding out experienced members of the staff and promoting newcomers rapidly. Soon, there was a cadre of new members of the manufacturing management staff with very limited experience who had become "Irwin's pets" (as the rest of the staff began to call them). Irwin referred to this group openly as "the keepers," and awarded them with stock options and trips on the company jet.

The extent of the pandering to the newcomers was significant, as was the turnover at the experienced level. Soon, the departure of experienced staff had so seriously weakened the operational capabilities of the manufacturing department that, as Frank said, "It's a good thing we're not trying to do the type of maintenance jobs that we used to . . . because we no longer have the capabilities."

Resolution

Mike, Don, and Frank concluded that the mismanagement was so pronounced and the annual activity reporting so distorted that Irwin had to

continued

be deriving personal financial benefit from the systematic understaffing, the cost cutting related to the deferral of necessary maintenance, and the overstatement of process-improvement dollar savings. They formed what they called the "Truth Team" and began a confidential fraud investigation. They obtained an ally in the human resources department, John Rivers, who was aware of the dysfunctional human resource symptoms that the manufacturing department had been displaying—favoritism and personnel manipulation.

When the Truth Team presented its hypothesis to Rivers, he provided them with a copy of Irwin's goals and objectives, the achievement of which were ultimately linked to incentive bonus payments and salary raises. The situation was just as they had expected: Irwin's performance bonus (which was significant) was dependent on only two performance metrics: first, the extent to which he could cut costs from a baseline budget, and second, the annual dollar savings reported for process improvements.

By manipulating the staff-level table and reported savings, and deferring necessary maintenance, Irwin had achieved windfall-profit personal performance bonuses of approximately $90,000 in each of the previous two years. This was a systematic manipulation that, given the dishonest estimates that went into the reported savings, constituted de facto fraud.

The necessary course of action became clear. Don, Mike, and John Rivers met with the management of the internal audit department. Audit Manager Dan Wood agreed with their interpretation. Senior Auditor Jose Rivera performed the necessary analysis to firm up the team's contentions about the before-and-after levels of maintenance and repairs and staffing, and the misreported construction-in-progress charges.

After senior management was informed about what had actually been happening, it was clear that Irwin could not continue in his current capacity. Moreover, his lack of ethics and basic honesty was a disqualification for any responsible position in the company. Consequently, he was terminated.

One conclusion is obvious: When the reporting of performance metrics is significantly distorted, the incentive compensation system may be the reason. There is also a more subtle lesson: Obvious favoritism and manipulation of staff through pandering and payoffs might be a symptom of underlying conflicts of interest. In such instances, the individual who is personally profiting by abusing a position of power is co-opting others through manipulation and dispensation of favors.

CHAPTER 6

Fraud against the Organization (Asset Misappropriation)

From a frequency standpoint, the majority of asset-misappropriation fraud will be employee fraud; however, from a total loss standpoint, management fraud will again predominate. As noted earlier, when managers commit asset-misappropriation fraud, the culprit will usually be administrative rather than operating management.

In the misappropriation categories, the symptoms of management fraud are often the same as those for employee fraud. Consequently, this chapter presents the symptoms without differentiating between the two types. In fact, the major differences between cases of management and of employee asset-misappropriation fraud are usually the size of the loss, the effect of positional authority on the fraud, and the scope of the activity.

This chapter first presents some general symptoms, then discusses those areas of asset misappropriation that are most likely to result in management fraud: vendor billing (shell company) schemes, other disbursement schemes, inventory and other assets, and diversion of receipts.

VARIOUS GENERAL ACCOUNTING-CYCLE FRAUD SYMPTOMS

The "Common Red Flags of Fraud" from the 1998 KPMG fraud study[1] are:

- Personal financial pressure
- Vices such as substance abuse and gambling
- Extravagant purchases or lifestyle
- Real or imagined grievances against the company or management

- Ongoing transactions with related parties
- Increased stress
- Internal pressure, including management pressure to meet budgets
- Short vacations and unexplained hours

These are good indicators that accounting-cycle-type fraud might be taking place in an organization. Extravagant lifestyle is a particularly strong red flag. Some of these symptoms may also be indicators of management fraud.

Some additional generic symptoms are:

- Clearance accounts with an excessive incidence of old, larger balances
- Rollovers of transactions from one clearance account to another to avoid analyses of accounts based on aging criteria, particularly when amounts are split (or combined) to avoid detection
- An unusual frequency of entries to clearance accounts from one source and/or unusual amounts (such as even "$000s" or cents, if that would be unusual)
- A pattern of consistent large inventory shortages in particular or, to a lesser extent, other variations of overstated inventory, which can be a symptom of multiple varieties of fraud (purchasing, unbilled sales, or management fraud)
- Unreconciled bank accounts either because reconciliations were not performed or there are large, recurring unlocated differences
- Various Benford's Law patterns (and/or excessive "$000s")

VENDOR BILLINGS—FALSE INVOICES/ PHANTOM VENDOR (SHELL COMPANIES)

Concept

Shell company billing schemes and fraudulent disbursements involve payment for fictitious goods or services to nonexistent companies, and they usually constitute management fraud. They are considered accounting-cycle transactional fraud, typically involving breakdowns in the internal control system when perpetrated by employees. As management fraud, they usually involve overrides of the control system.

These are disbursement rather than purchasing types of fraud, and they differ from conflict-of-interest fraud in that the latter usually involves real transactions for which the profitability has been altered (e.g., ongoing purchases from a middleman company at inflated rates), whereas vendor billing fraud is typically based on nonexistent transactions.

Discussion

As noted, shell company billing schemes are usually management fraud and may involve operating as well as administrative management. In the 1996 ACFE report,[2] the median loss from shell company billing fraud was $590,000, indicating that most of these instances of fraud would have been perpetrated by management rather than by employees.

Although collusion is always helpful, employee fraud is frequently a lone-wolf venture and entails avoidance of preventive controls. The longer-term success of such fraud depends on the ability to avoid detection. As *Occupational Fraud and Abuse*[3] points out, purchases of services rather than goods are a common method of avoiding detection through inventory shortages.

In addition to the greater positional opportunity, avoidance of detection is the extra edge that a perpetrator of management fraud brings to the table in this area. Usually, in management fraud of this type, the individual responsible for detection is the one who is the primary beneficiary. Frequently, the responsibility for detection involves some aspect of budgetary oversight and review, such as cost or profit center accountability.

The case study in this section gives an example of a situation in which the perpetrator is also the person responsible for budgetary oversight. Obviously, when this occurs, detection is considerably less likely.

Symptoms

As is usually the case in the misappropriation categories, the symptoms of management fraud will typically be the same as those of employee fraud. Please note that, in this area, the symptoms may also reflect the existence of conflict-of-interest fraud.

- Excessive incidence of disbursements being miscoded to a dumping-ground black hole in the P&L structure, such as where sundry credits are available to offset and obscure the effect of the debit.

- Incongruous account coding of disbursements, particularly when field operating units are providing the coding. "Incongruous" means that a charge that clearly should go to one activity is charged to another—for example, payments to a hardware vendor being charged as an entertainment expense. While this is usually a symptom of employee-level disbursement fraud, it could also be a symptom of management fraud.

- A variation on the preceding symptom whereby there is an excessive incidence of amounts being charged to "miscellaneous" or "sundry expense." Such cases are more likely to constitute management fraud, particularly if the debit dumping-ground symptom is present.

- A pattern of deficient documentation, particularly when this would be uncharacteristic, for a vendor or class of transactions.

- Generic company names and/or names that are very close to established, well-known companies, such as "BCD company" or "Intell."

- Variations on or extensions of the preceding symptom: vendors whose existence cannot be verified or established by third-party evidence, for example, vendors that are not listed in the phone book, for whom D&Bs cannot be obtained, or for whom nominee owners are listed.

- A pattern of substantial payments to one company for essentially unverifiable services, particularly when these payments reflect considerable budget overruns.

- The classic area of unverifiable services is consulting services. Look for a pattern of payments to consultants whose identity cannot be established or for which the services to be rendered are dubious and/or vague.

- Payments to related parties (or associates) for unverifiable goods or services. The key is recognizing the related party. One fraud audit technique is to obtain names of potential recipients of fraudulent payments from employment applications (e.g., references) or personnel records. Surprisingly, something as obvious as a wife's maiden name was actually the key to one management fraud that the author investigated.

- Disbursements processed out of the mainstream processing routines, particularly when this involves avoidance of setting up a vendor in the master vendor file. The tip-off might be manual checks for recurring payments. This symptom is an excellent way to identify shell companies. In the old days—before the microfilming of vendor records—savvy auditors used the "sundry vendor" files as fertile hunting grounds to identify recurring payments for which the vendor should have been set up but wasn't.

- Uncharacteristic treatment of one particular company, such as early payment to one vendor when all others are paid in 45 days. Examine the underlying relationship.

- Vendor invoice numbers running in sequence. This is an indicator of shell company fraud, which in turn indicates a bogus vendor—or one that sells only to your company. A variation on this is clumsily prepared invoices.

- A readily recognizable vendor invoice template—exactly the same format used for invoices obviously prepared on a PC—used repetitively for what should be different vendors. This is an indication that the same individual is preparing purported vendor invoices for what should be different vendors. In addition to format, similar numerical sequences, descriptions, and other invoice components are tip-offs. This practice is fairly easy to recognize.

- A pattern of missing receiving documentation. This can be construed as a symptom of fraud only when missing documentation is an unusual circumstance in an organization. For many companies, unfortunately, it's not.

- Excessive scrap rates.

- Excessive local selection of vendors or freight carriers other than the approved vendors, particularly when uneconomical rates are charged.

- Multiple instances of identical addresses, particularly P.O. boxes, in disbursement records.

- A vendor address that matches an employee address (after elimination of "travel expense").

- A vendor bank account number that matches an employee bank account number.

- A pattern of multiple endorsements on disbursement checks, particularly if the last endorsement is common to all checks.

- A change in a vendor address in the master file, followed by a change back to the original address after a short period of time.

- Vendor invoices that are consistently just below the limit that would require a higher level of approval (or some variation of avoidance of more stringent handling). A classic example of analogous circumvention is consistent unsupported expense report charges for $24.XX when charges over $25 require support.

- A variation on the preceding symptom: invoice splitting or unbundling, whereby, instead of preparing one invoice for X amount, two (or more) invoices will be prepared for X/2 to circumvent approval requirements.

- Another variation on the preceding symptom: splitting contracts to circumvent competitive bidding requirements.

- Inappropriate charges to balance sheet accounts, particularly construction in progress, and most especially maintenance-type charges.

- Substantial purchase overruns in areas that are not susceptible to physical verification—for example, underground tanks or dirt for fill—particularly when coupled with AFE switching or rollovers to hide the extent of the overruns.

- Excessive payments to "fuzzy" areas of accountability, such as consulting or advertising. This is analogous to the preceding symptom. In that case, physical verification was difficult; in this case, verification of actual services performed is difficult.

- A responsible purchasing individual, such as a manager, agent, or supervisor, uncharacteristically handling all matters pertaining to a certain vendor or class of vendors, particularly those that would normally be taken care of by the administrative support staff.

- A vendor sales rep making frequent recurring visits with no apparent business reason to a purchasing agent or buyer.

TIP OF THE ICEBERG

Our company has a well-established protocol for corporate security and law. Our audit director refers to our security protocol as the "old Army football team approach: Mr. Inside and Mr. Outside." As the phrase implies, Internal Audit handles those inside aspects of a fraud investigation such as employee interviews, records, and data analysis. Security gets involved with the external aspects such as interviewing nonemployees, interfacing with various agencies, and obtaining public information.

Our company is in the pharmaceutical industry, so we use outside technical consultants extensively, particularly in the area of research and development (R&D). Recently, Audit Supervisor Delray Johnson got a call from Security relative to one such technical consulting company.

Security had received a hot-line call from an individual who claimed to be a former employee. This individual advised them to "look at the Red Company" but was unwilling to provide his name. He did allege that the ownership of Red Company was one of our employees but was unwilling to provide any more details.

Delray looked up this company on the vendor master payment file and found nothing particularly out of the ordinary. Based on their invoices, the Red Company appeared to be a small technical-consulting company specializing in microbiology. Our company had paid them approximately $175,000 over a three-year period.

Based on the accounting distribution of the charges, all the work would have been performed on various R&D projects. Interestingly enough, the charges to individual projects were relatively insignificant compared to the total expenditures on those projects. Payments had been mailed to a post office box address; however, this was far from unusual.

Security had some time available that week and followed up with the U.S. Post Office. Surprise! The individual who had opened that P.O. box was Jim Nelson, manager of the technical lab. Nelson reported directly to the vice president of research and development. Delray examined the microfilm records of the underlying support for the particular payments to Red Company and, to nobody's surprise, they had all been approved by Nelson.

continued

Delray was well aware of the process: The manager of the lab awarded all contracts based on technical specs, oversaw the work, and approved all invoices for payment. This individual was also primarily responsible for establishing the project budget, both the preparation of the estimated total, and the responsibility for performance reporting against the budget. All of the payments to Red Company had been charged to multiyear projects and, as indicated, these were fairly inconsequential when compared to the total amounts authorized for those projects.

Delray discussed Nelson with his superior, the VP of R&D (who, Delray later said, had the demeanor of "a mad scientist"). This individual didn't appear terribly interested in the mundane aspects of budgets and accounting for expenditures. Moreover, he was relatively new to the company. The VP did say that Nelson was an excellent performer and that he had apparently come into some money—he drove an expensive Porsche, had acquired an upscale new house, and "supported his wife's 'antiques business,'" which seemed to be more of a hobby than a moneymaker."

Delray looked up Red Company in the phone book and could find no such company listed. Moreover, he checked with a professional association and found no record of the company, nor the individuals listed on the company letterhead. Based on what Security had determined, it seemed that Nelson was the recipient of $175,000 in apparently fraudulent payments. Delray made the offhand observation that Nelson's wife could get a lot of antiques for that . . . but could Nelson get a Porsche and a large house?

Security and Delray interviewed Nelson and confronted him with what had been determined. Nelson was forthcoming; he acknowledged what he had done and appeared to show genuine remorse. As an experienced fraud investigator, however, Delray thought that Nelson "rolled over a little too easily." Consequently, he demanded authorization from him to obtain all of his personal bank records as well as those of Red Company.

When Delray followed through with the bank, he quickly recognized that there was significantly more money coming into Nelson's personal account than would be explained by Red Company alone. He obtained microfilm copies of the deposits and saw the rest of the story.

Approximately $550,000 that did not come from Red Company was deposited in Nelson's personal account over a three-year period. At this point, Delray had a pretty good idea of what he would see when he looked at the microfilm copies of the specific deposit details.

His expectation was correct. The payees were all larger, well-established consulting companies that had done a substantial amount of recurring technical work for the lab over the three-year period. Delray and Security contacted these companies.

The companies claimed they "had to play ball" in order to get major contracts with our company for significant R&D projects. They maintained that Nelson told them to invoice the company separately for "his share" in an amount determined by him. Nelson would then approve the payment to them, and they would complete the cycle by issuing payment to him in the same amount. It was the checks drawn on these companies' accounts that Nelson deposited in his account.

Delray compared the amounts deposited in Nelson's account with payments made by our company to the respective vendors and was able to account for all of the $550,000 of the round-trip payments.

Based on the well-documented case, a court-ordered restitution plan was obtained. Nelson sold his upscale house and car, and eventually disposed of his wife's antiques collection to pay the majority of the $725,000 total. Delray reports that he has made all the scheduled payments since then.

There is a punch line associated with this case. The identity of the hot-line informant eventually became known. It turned out that he was the former VP of R&D who had left the company 18 months previously under a bit of a cloud. This individual had been having an office affair with his administrative assistant, which indirectly led to his departure. In the intervening period, he had obtained a divorce from his wife and had recently married the administrative assistant. Delray's take on the situation was that the former VP of R&D knew all along that something was not right with Red Company—but only recently became free to act.

OTHER DISBURSEMENT FRAUD

Concept

As distinct from shell company billing schemes and fraudulent disbursements involving payment for fictitious goods or services to nonexistent companies, other types of disbursement fraud typically (but not exclusively) involve misdirection of otherwise valid disbursements. Perhaps they should be called "quasi-valid" disbursements because initiation of a second payment of a valid receipt of goods, for the purpose of misappropriating the return check from the vendor, is also an example of this classification, although perpetrated by an employee rather than by management.

Since instances of this type of fraud typically involve payment of otherwise valid charges, they may not leave a telltale debit behind that would subject them to P&L scrutiny, and, consequently, they do not require that management look the other way.

Discussion

In general, these types of disbursements are more likely to be employee fraud rather than management fraud. Those that constitute management fraud typically involve technical or administrative management.

As is apparent from the symptoms of this type of fraud, many instances involve using positional authority to get specialized transactions through the disbursement system. This includes transactions such as escheat payments and customer refunds. Variations of this nature, which typically involve administrative management, are our focus here. Examples of other disbursement-type fraud as perpetrated by management include:

- Diversion of escheatable funds.
- Diversion of customer credit balances.
- Using clearance accounts—that is, "suspense" accounts—to "park" telltale debits resulting from improper disbursements, and then manipulating the amounts to avoid detection.
- Directing the debit offsets to fraudulent disbursements to sundry other asset accounts that are not regularly analyzed or that involve realization and collectibility issues such that subsequent write-off is not unusual. Examples of this type of account are various claims for price support programs, cooperative advertising, or defective merchandise.

Note that the first two examples would not impact the bottom line and would therefore avoid P&L scrutiny. The third and fourth examples might eventually impact the bottom line but in such a roundabout fashion that the accountability would be obscured.

Symptoms

As with vendor billing and other misappropriation-type fraud, the symptoms of management fraud are typically the same as those of employee fraud.

- An absence of escheated funds, or, in a variation, a pattern of last-minute resolution prior to the escheat deadline.

- Disposition of customer credits to a party other than the initial payer. The ability to initiate these typically implies at least supervisory responsibility.

- A variation on the preceding symptom: patterns of offsetting unrelated excess credit balances, such as customer overpayments, against sundry debits, such as bad debt write-offs. This permits the canceling of otherwise telltale debits.

- Another variation on the preceding symptom: issuance of payment against dormant credit balances resulting from customer overpayments, particularly if timed to occur shortly before the funds would become escheatable.

- A pattern of debits to clearance accounts for which the related credits are to cash. This is similar to the preceding symptom in that it constitutes misappropriation of funds or disbursement fraud. (This is based on the assumption that sundry debits can be buried in clearance accounts that are not analyzed.) Pay particular attention if there is a subsequent pattern of rollovers to other clearance or suspense accounts.

- Clearance accounts with an excessive incidence of old, larger balances, which is an indication of fraudulent debits being parked.

- Rollovers of transactions from one clearance account to another, to avoid analyses of accounts based on aging criteria, particularly when amounts are split or combined to avoid detection.

- An unusual frequency of entries to clearance accounts from one source and/or unusual amounts, such as even 000s or cents, if that would be unusual.

- An excessive number of checks returned to the preparer for mailing. This is typically employee rather than management fraud.

CASE STUDY

OTHER DISBURSEMENTS—THE HANDS-ON CONTROLLER

In conducting the audit of a stand-alone subsidiary, John Green recognized that there was definitely a problem, but he wasn't sure what it meant. The general ledger accounts receivable balance was $240,000 over the subledger, and this unreconcilable difference had existed for more than one year.

John discovered that the former controller, James Harris (who was thoroughly disliked by the accounting staff because of his excessively hands-on approach and generally disagreeable attitude), left the company around the time that this unreconcilable difference initially appeared, about eleven months previously. Since that time, this difference had remained basically constant.

On looking further into this situation, John discovered that the difference was only relatively recently recognized: The former controller himself had evidently been performing the accounts receivable control account reconciliation to the supporting subledger, but this had not been retained on file. Since they had not been performing this, the accounting staff had not been aware of the difference, nor did they recognize that the reconciliation was not on file until some time after the controller's departure.

Once it was recognized that the reconciliations were missing, the accounting staff proved their diligence and went back two and a half years to prepare them. In addition to the constant difference for the eleven months after Harris's departure, the records indicated a steady buildup for the 18-month period leading up to his departure.

John first validated the general ledger control account totals by margin analyses, which indicated that the control account was in line with sales and collections. He considered the steady buildup in the difference to be indicative of possible manipulation.

He focused on the internal controls to determine what might have gone wrong. He discovered that the controls over incoming receipts and issuance of credit memos were quite good. Based on John's conversation with the individual who maintained the accounts receivable subledger, however, one curiosity did emerge.

There was a relatively high incidence of customer credit balances, which the receivables clerk said was due to the nature of the business. Evidently, many customers were on extended payment plans that involved fixed monthly charges with a variable component. The unusual practice was that the subsidiary never issued checks to the customers to return the overpayments. Rather, in accordance with the instructions of the former controller, the receivables clerk would offset the customer credits against other customers' uncollectible balances. As a result, the subsidiary's reported bad debt experience was zero.

Neither practice—not issuing refund checks and the bad debt off-sets—was in accordance with established company procedures, so John's curiosity was piqued. Next, he discovered another example of Harris's hands-on approach. Harris performed the bank reconciliations—and would not let the accounting staff see the canceled checks. The accounting staff regarded their lack of access to the canceled checks as a manifestation of Harris's lack of trust for them, but John saw it as something else.

Using the audit software Audit Command Language (ACL), he obtained a list of all credit entries to cash that had a debit to accounts receivable. For the 24 months prior to Harris's departure, these averaged about $13,000 per month—but there were none since he had left. According to the check register, the payees were various customers, and the sundry check request documentation generated by Harris indicated "To pay customer's credit balance."

John knew what he would find when he examined the canceled checks. Sure enough, these bore second endorsements to a "James Company." Corporate security followed up with the state agency responsible for incorporation records and discovered that the owner of James Company was none other than the former controller, James Harris. It was clear what had been happening: Harris had been causing checks to be issued to credit-balance customers, intercepting the checks, and converting them to his personal use.

The story had a happy ending. Harris had invested the misappropriated funds and was able to make restitution. He received a relatively light sentence . . . and the office staff threw a party to celebrate their good fortune in not having to work for such a petty tyrant anymore.

INVENTORY

Concept

Fraudulent financial statements are generally classified as fraud for the company; however, inventory overstatements are frequently also used to facilitate management fraud *against* the company. Overstated inventory can provide a cushion to cover excess charges or lost profits elsewhere in the financials and to obscure overall P&L accountability to facilitate major management fraud.

In addition to overstating inventory to conceal the effect of misappropriations elsewhere, non-financial-statement management fraud in the inventory area might involve physical movement to a third party and subsequent loss (with no prospect of recovery), pledging fictitious inventory as collateral, or similar activity. Operating-management fraud in the inventory area usually involves leveraging relationships and is typically off the books. It could as readily be classified as conflict-of-interest corruption-type fraud. These activities invariably result in residual (overstated) balances.

Discussion

Prior to the rash of revenue-related financial-reporting fraud in the early 2000s, inventory fraud was historically the most common type of financial-statement fraud, because of the relative ease of committing it. In the study of fraudulent financial reporting published in 1999, the Treadway Commission's Committee of Sponsoring Organizations (COSO)[4] reported that overstated assets represented almost 50 percent of the cases. The majority of these asset overstatements involved inventory.

Interestingly enough, the 1998 KPMG[5] study (see Appendix E) indicates a significant extent of management fraud in this area. Specifically, this area has the highest average loss for misappropriations ($346,000) and a relatively high incidence (43 reporting companies).[6] Considering the amount of the average loss, a majority of these instances would be expected to have resulted from management fraud.

Nonmanagement non-financial-statement inventory fraud is usually some variation of employee theft characterized by large unexplained inventory shortages, particularly of inventory that has resale value. This can be very profitable for the perpetrators if the merchandise is a controlled substance or is usable in black market operations.

As with payroll, the major threat in the inventory area is "ghosts"—that is, fictitious goods, typically accounted for by overstating physical inventory quantities. In addition to overstated quantities, inventory can be manipulated using a variety of methods, including manipulating cutoffs relative to related sales and/or accruals, adjusting entries to the books, overstating inventory costs, including consigned goods, and failing to reflect obsolescence.

The primary financial audit techniques applicable to this area include analytical procedures, physical inventory observations, and review of the soundness of the cost system. The primary fraud investigative techniques involve determining the identity of third parties and the actual physical location of inventory movement. In this latter regard, external bills of lading can be particularly useful.

Symptoms

Symptoms involving overstated quantities/values include:

- Symptoms detectable by analytical procedures such as comparisons to other periods or companies, obscuring that margins are too high or the cost of sales is too low, inventory increases disproportionate to sales, or inventory levels that change disproportionately to other metrics like inventory turnover, inventory as a percentage of total assets, or shipping costs as a percentage of inventory.

- Alteration of physical inventory count sheets or *double-counting*.

- Cutoffs for physical inventory counts and sales or liabilities at different dates.

- Accounting journal entries that inflate inventory value.

- Obsolescence not reflected.

- Overstatement of inventory costs, such as improperly including selling, general, and administrative (SG&A) costs or manipulation of last-in, first-out (LIFO) reserves.

- Inclusion of goods to which the company does not have title—for example, consignments.

Symptoms of basic inventory misappropriation fraud include:

- Shipments of excessive quantities to a third-party, who then declares bankruptcy. This is the classic symptom of this type of fraud. Additional tip-offs include the third party's obvious lack of creditworthiness and other overrides of prudent practice, suspicious timing such as an escalation of shipments just before bankruptcy, and similar practices. This symptom indicates management fraud.

- Large unexplained inventory shortages, particularly of inventory that has resale value. This is a symptom of employee theft (but see below).
- Nonexistent inventory pledged as collateral.

A third type of symptom of inventory-related fraud involves a pattern of consistent, large inventory shortages in particular or, to a lesser extent, other variations of overstated inventory. This can indicate other varieties of fraud, such as purchasing or unbilled sales, or management fraud.

CASE STUDY

DIVERTED INVENTORY LEADS TO BANKRUPTCY

Subsidiary Audit: Resignation and Bankruptcy

Audit Manager Sally Gull was getting ready for an audit of a subsidiary in Florida when she discovered that this was not going to be a routine event. The general manager of the subsidiary had suddenly resigned, and a major customer, Pestisol, had just gone bankrupt, leaving the company with a $1.7 million bad debt. Sally wondered whether these seemingly unrelated events might be connected.

She was not surprised to hear about the abrupt resignation of the subsidiary's general manager, William "Buck" Terwilliger. The subsidiary had been acquired a couple years previously—Terwilliger had formerly been the sole proprietor, and Sally had heard that he was chafing under what he described as "large company bureaucracy." Sally's take on the topic was that any arrangement that had Terwilliger working for anyone else would likely be unsatisfactory for "Buck."

Sally's company produced agricultural pesticides and sold to a variety of customers, ranging from farming cooperatives to medium-sized distributors. Pestisol was one of the larger accounts; however, Sally recognized one peculiarity: How had it qualified for a large enough line of credit to be able to incur a $1.7 million bad debt? Pestisol had only recently gone into business; worse, Jimbo Rogers, the owner/operator, had a history of business failures, including one prior bankruptcy.

The audit team in the field was experienced, and they quickly went to work. Lead auditor Jonathan Ford checked shipments to Pestisol. He discovered a significant pattern:

- Pestisol had been extended unusually long credit terms: 90 days, as opposed to the customary 30-day terms provided all other accounts.
- Pestisol had been granted only a $500,000 line of credit. Shipments were made over that limit because Buck Terwilliger overrode the credit manager (as general manager, Buck had that authority) and approved continuing shipments.
- The particular shipments were directly to former customers, not to Pestisol.

The timing of the shipments was particularly interesting. Pestisol had actually never made any payments: The company declared bankruptcy shortly after the first payments would have been due under the extended 90-day terms. More important, the pace of the shipments escalated markedly near the end: $1.2 million (the amount in excess of the established line of credit) was shipped in the last two weeks.

Jonathan reported to Sally: "It gets curiouser and curiouser. . . . Two days after Pestisol declared bankruptcy, general manager Buck Terwilliger suddenly resigned." The audit team decided to contact the former customers that had been the recipients of the direct shipments.

These were largely small farming co-ops, and they supplied the missing link: They had been provided deep discounts (20 percent off) if they remitted in cash within 10 days to Pestisol.

By now, you can guess what really happened. The bankruptcy of Pestisol had been preplanned, and this had been arranged between Buck and Jimbo, who turned out to be good friends of long standing. Their scheme was to split the cash proceeds between themselves and declare bankruptcy, leaving the company holding the bag.

The resolution of this matter, as is typically the case in such issues, was the proverbial half-full glass. A substantial, but not full, recovery was negotiated from Buck, and the company chalked this one up as a learning experience.

SKIMMING/CASH RECEIPT MISAPPROPRIATION FRAUD

Concept

It is debatable whether cash receipt fraud even belongs in a discussion of management fraud. This type of fraud entails the lowest median loss (skimming: $50,000[7]) of the categories included in this book as management fraud against the organization.

The key concept for the person committing the fraud is to work around the recorded accountability represented by the open receivable that relates to the diverted proceeds. Typically, the receivable is subsequently cleared by a credit memo, a journal entry, or misapplication of an unrelated cash receipt. To that end, this is considered more of an accounting-cycle fraud in that its continued viability depends on on-the-books transactions (albeit deceptive ones).

The opportunity to systematically wipe out large amounts of receivables while keeping the effect of the offsets from showing up on the P&L would take it to the next level and make it a management fraud. Alternatively, if the fraud perpetrator has access to sundry revenue for which the receivable has not yet been recorded, the fraud is much more easily committed. Continuing concealment, however, depends on keeping others from recognizing the missing sundry revenue.

Discussion

As previously indicated, most diverted-receipts schemes constitute employee rather than management fraud. It can be illustrative to contrast a typical "lapping" fraud with a management-type diverted-receipts fraud to highlight the differences between employee and management fraud in this area.

The first fraud that the author was ever involved with was a lapping case. As in all such cases, the perpetrator's problem was that she was actually "borrowing" rather than stealing from the company. She was dependent on a continuing stream of receipts that could be misapplied against earlier diverted receipts, day after day. However, she had to keep robbing Peter to pay Paul, as it were, and would never have gotten ahead of the game.

In this case, however, she discovered how to permanently wipe out the open receivables. She had access to receipts for sundry revenue for which the receivable had not yet been recorded. Bingo! She was home free.

She would take a check for $5,000 payable to the company (which would have been difficult for her to convert because of its size) and record it as, say, fifty $100 payments. This would wipe out the open receivables relating to numerous small payments that she had been able to divert to her personal account. Because the $5,000 sundry revenue had not initially been recorded, there was no open receivable remaining after the diversion. Using this approach, she was able to permanently divert more than $110,000, until the profit center manager recognized the revenue shortfall, because the sundry revenue was no longer being recorded.

Consider an alternative scenario: Instead of being the cash receipts clerk, this woman is the profit center manager. Assume further that, because of her more exalted organizational status, she is now able to convert the $5,000 in sundry revenue checks to her personal account (see the next case study). Now she is able to divert the proceeds without a telltale debit or an open receivable on the books. And, as the profit center manager, she is responsible for the operating profit analysis. She is now able to leverage her positional authority to accomplish more and go undetected. That's basically how management fraud in this area works.

Symptoms

As is the case in the misappropriation categories, the symptoms of management fraud are typically the same as the symptoms of employee fraud:

- Write-offs of amounts built up in clearance accounts as a result of cash sales.

- An inexplicably high incidence of cancellations of sales orders.

- A marked drop in sundry revenue (e.g., scrap sales), particularly when recorded accountability has not been established.

- A marked (and disproportionate) reduction in rebates received.

- Customers remitting locally (or to credit) that should not be—for example, major customers that are not credit-critical. Look for credit memos or other write-offs.

- A pattern of credit memos coupled with the preceding symptom. Look for patterns of large recurring credits by particular customers (specifically, customers who remit locally) or by the initiator.

- A buildup of deposits in transit on bank reconciliations. This is a symptom of possible lapping and occurs when a company sends monthly statements to its customers. The person engaged in lapping must get the open (lapped but not yet covered) credits reflected in the customers' accounts. The simple way to do this is to record the offsetting debit as a cash deposit in transit.

- The absence of any cash currency (or total cash currency on deposit less than $1.00). This is a symptom of diverted receipts and/or lapping. A variation on this is using the amount of cash currency as the plug figure to balance the total required.

- The composition of bank deposits at variance with the coding of the deposit slip. This is a special audit procedure that would require intercepting the deposit or obtaining a microfilm record of the deposit. Although an unusual procedure, this should be undertaken if other symptoms of lapping are present. If a difference in the composition of the deposit is detected, this is a reasonably sure sign of lapping or cash receipts fraud.

CASE STUDY

CASH RECEIPTS FRAUD—THE VIPER

Beginning

Mark O'Malley, audit manager for Acme Farm Equipment, was surprised when the credit manager, Terry Wilson, suddenly showed up at O'Malley's office and said, "Help me out with this. Something looks strange at the Midwestern Region."

Mark knew that the Midwestern Region had been plagued by unusually poor agings of receivables as compared to the other Acme regions, but the ultimate collectibility of the receivables (as measured by bad debt experience) was curiously better than that of the other regions. Although this was anomalous, the feeling at headquarters was that "if it wasn't broke, why fix it?"

Wilson dropped photocopies of two checks on Mark's desk. The checks—one for $10,500 and another for $14,500—were from a substantial customer and were payable to Acme. The checks had not been deposited in Acme's lockbox account, however; in fact, they had apparently not been deposited in an Acme bank account at all. Instead, they had been rather crudely endorsed to a company called Ace Software, an organization in no way affiliated with Acme. The checks had been deposited on October 4 in Ace Software's account at the same bank used by the Midwestern Region.

Terry said, "I received these check copies from the customer in response to my follow-up on invoices that were overdue at the time I called. Since that time, however, large credits totaling $25,000 were posted to the account on October 28, so the invoices are not overdue anymore." The customer also told Wilson that instead of remitting to the lockbox, they had been paying locally at the direction of Credit Supervisor Glen Ogleby, who was based in the Midwestern Region office.

As if this weren't puzzling enough, Wilson went on to say that this was the second such incident that he'd encountered wherein a customer provided photocopies of checks that had evidently been endorsed to Ace Software and deposited in the non-Acme bank account about three weeks prior to the date indicated as the payment date in Acme's receivable records.

Initial Analysis—Development of Hypothesis

Mark recognized what the preceding symptoms could mean and set about systematically developing his hypothesis. First, he reviewed the last audit conducted at the Midwestern Region headquarters. Sure enough, one of the audit findings was that certain customers were being instructed to remit to the headquarters credit function rather than to the lockbox. The justification offered was that this permitted deliveries sooner than would be the case if the customers remitted in the ordinary way to the lockbox. The internal audit report action plan indicated this practice would be severely curtailed, but obviously that hadn't happened.

Mark suspected that the audit finding was only part of the control weakness. He followed up and discovered that his guess was correct: Not only was the credit department receiving checks, they were actually applying the cash—in other words, coding the receipts for credit to the customers' receivable records. This was clearly incompatible with standard segregation of duties, but the relatively inexperienced audit team had missed that.

Mark then checked out his next guess: Could the credit supervisor issue credit memos? He was relieved to discover that this was not the case. So, while the ability to receive checks and direct the accounting for these checks was bad enough, Mark thought that the worst thing that could be happening was lapping. After all, the bad debt experience was good, so the checks were presumably eventually finding their way to the bank, right?

continued

Well, Mark was a savvy old-timer. He knew that lapping, if that were the case here, was relatively benign, so his concern would be something more substantial. He also knew that Glen Ogleby had been rumored to have come into a substantial inheritance. The middle-aged Ogleby had acquired a Dodge Viper and a downtown penthouse, and rumor had it that Ogleby was "living large." (Mark was amused when he heard this because he knew Ogleby from way back and had always thought that Ogleby needed to get a life—previously, he had spent way too much time in the office.)

Mark knew where to look next. He knew that Acme's farm equipment business had a profitable sideline: In addition to the month-to-month rentals of heavy equipment, which comprised 95 percent of their business, they also installed ancillary smaller equipment for heating hen-houses at smaller farms. Over the years, this business had dwindled, but it was nevertheless highly profitable. It was now so sporadic, however, that Acme accounted for this as sundry revenue.

Mark knew that the controls over this sideline business were relatively weak. Most notably, because it was so sporadic, the sundry revenue was recorded essentially on a cash basis—that is, not until it was collected. When Mark checked the comparative P&L for the Midwestern Region, he confirmed his hunch: Over the past three years, the sundry revenue for this aspect of the Midwestern Region had declined 80 percent. He checked with a sales rep whom he knew from way back; the rep said business was as good as ever.

Validating the Hypothesis

Mark thought there was a possibility that lapping was occurring, coupled with diversion of the receipts for sundry revenue. He did not want to contact the customers directly at this point, however.

How to proceed? Mark was shrewd. He knew a sure test to spot lapping: Get copies from the bank's microfilm records demonstrating what actually comprised the daily deposits for a few days and compare that to the internal cash application details. Initially, he selected deposits for 10 days and requested the bank microfilm records. He had to agree that Acme would pay the overtime charges in order to get this on an expedited basis.

The bank records confirmed his hypothesis: Lapping was occurring for the receipts received in the headquarters office, in combination with diversion of sundry receipts to wipe out the otherwise open receivables. The consistent pattern that emerged left no doubt; the only questions remaining were: Who else was involved, if anyone (Mark had determined that Ogleby prepared the bank deposit and received and coded the larger checks)? How long had this been going on? How much had been stolen? (At least one Viper, Mark thought to himself).

Mark also could not resist a little gamesmanship. He called Ogleby and asked him, "Where is the off-books record that you had to be keeping?" Mark knew that a lapper has to keep a scratch-sheet record of which accounts are still open at any time. Ogleby, of course, responded with a churlish remark

When the audit team finished their analysis, the following facts were determined:

- Because he personally received and prepared the deposit, took it to the bank, and coded the larger checks for cash application, Ogleby was the only individual involved.

- To nobody's surprise, Ace Software was owned by Ogleby.

- Ogleby had actually diverted enough to purchase several Vipers (and more than a couple downtown condos). Three years ago, as is typical of such fraud, he started slowly by diverting approximately $65,000, but this quickly escalated to $225,000 the next year, and then $1.1 million.

The party was now over for Ogleby. Given the magnitude of the fraud, management elected to prosecute, and Ogleby was convicted in an open-and-shut case. Mark visited Ogleby's office after he was gone and found the scratch sheet. Ogleby had attempted to delete the records from his PC, but he had not written over them—they were easily reconstructed and a complete record that tied into the bank records was available.

CHAPTER 7

Fraud for the Organization

FINANCIAL REPORTING

Concept

Usually, significant fraudulent financial reporting begins at the top of the organization. The Treadway Commission's Committee of Sponsoring Organizations (COSO) 1999 report on 11 years of fraudulent financial reporting indicated that the CEO and/or CFO were involved in 83 percent of the instances of fraudulent financial reporting covered in that study.[1]

The significance of this observation is that fraudulent financial reporting by management does not normally result from a breakdown in the internal accounting control system. Rather, senior management uses positional leverage to, in essence, overpower the established control system. The implication is that substantive audit work directed at the top level is necessary to provide reasonable assurance against enterprise financial-reporting fraud. This top-level work should be twofold: recurring forensic reviews of specific financial areas and a focus on corporate governance.

In addition, senior management fraudulent financial reporting, ostensibly *for* the organization, with its concomitant questionable "tone at the top," is related to operating-management fraud *against* the organization. Although this book classifies it as fraud for the organization, fraudulent reporting typically favors the senior management individual(s) who direct such schemes.

As the preface to this book notes: "To consider one element of management fraud more important than the other is to miss the point: Major management fraud is all about leveraging positional power and is an interrelated top-down phenomenon—fraud for the organization leads to fraud against the organization, and vice versa."

The perception by operating management of fraud and corruption at the top of the organization will lead almost inevitably to fraud against the organization by this stratum of management. Over time, such fraud against the organization constitutes the source of the greatest potential for loss to the organization. While the Enron scandal first manifested itself as fraudulent financial reporting, it was primarily a "massive breach of trust," according to the Business Roundtable. As such, it opened the door for self-serving conflicts of interest. [Note: This was written before the self-serving conflicts of interest actually surfaced; however, they were predictable.]

As the following discussion elucidates, the most effective audit approach to recognize and detect—and thereby deter—senior management fraudulent financial reporting is top-level continuous monitoring using the power of information technology, coupled with forensic procedures. To be effective, this requires committing substantial computing resources, which can be further justified by synergistically also addressing operational indicia of corruption and conflict of interest.

Discussion

Much of what have been referred to as the corporate accounting scandals amounted to excessively aggressive, dubious, and misleading accounting rather than outright fraud. Very simply, the generally accepted accounting principles (GAAP) are unclear in many areas—for example, revenue recognition, where approximately 150 often contradictory and not conceptually consistent standards existed. This is not to minimize the crisis of confidence in U.S. financial reporting, which by now may have receded to a level of skepticism rather than distrust; rather, it is intended to provide context for the internal audit function.

The issue for internal audit is one of corporate *accountability* more than corporate *accounting*. The assurance role relative to the system of controls and forensic analyses of activities at the top are an important aspect of this. As internal auditors develop enhanced monitoring techniques to meet Sarbanes-Oxley requirements, we have a significant opportunity to kill two birds with one stone.

The real-time aspect of some requirements, such as certain aspects of the quarterly disclosures, can best be addressed by a powerful expansion of information-technology-driven continuous monitoring. Significantly, this enhanced analysis can identify fraudulent financial-reporting symptoms *and* operational symptoms of management corruption and conflict-of-interest fraud. Refer to "Middlemen/Related Parties" and "Top-Down Forensic Monitoring" in Chapter 9 for some basic examples.

As this was being written, public confidence in the U.S. capital markets and financial-reporting system had been seriously shaken. So many people had lost so much money, and the abuses of CEOs were so apparent, that there was a media feeding frenzy to drag the scoundrels off in the tumbrels. However, the crisis of confidence derived from a much broader problem than that of actual fraudulent financial reporting. As noted, misleading rather than fraudulent financial reporting was the primary problem. Related to that, the credibility of the certified public accountant (CPA) attest function had been seriously (and rightfully) eroded.

Mortimer B. Zuckerman, editor in chief of *U.S. News & World Report,* remarked: "The problem wasn't just what was illegal. It was what was *legal.* Accountants went about 'selling' creative tax avoidance and creative financing structures, using the GAAP rules to structure transactions that formally complied with the rules but lacked a true business purpose, all to maximize perceived earnings and minimize perceived debt."[2]

The magnitude of the rewards conflicted with—and in some cases corrupted—the system of financial reporting and corporate governance. In his "infectious greed" speech, Alan Greenspan said that the latter half of the 1990s provided "an outsized increase in opportunities for avarice."

The perceived abuses and excesses were very real. The stock market bubble demanded growth that would justify the exorbitant share prices. CEOs were rewarded excessively, and the envelope of financial reporting was stretched, in some cases, beyond the point of elasticity. In retrospect, the GAAP standards that should have provided a framework for meaningful financial reporting had been allowed to become too comfortable.

Make no mistake: The perception that the public accounting profession basically abdicated its fiduciary role is well founded. The fundamental problem, according to Baruch Lev in the *Wall Street Journal,* is that "GAAP conformity is intended by accountants to limit professional obligations and liability" rather than "provide a true and fair reflection of a company's business performance".[3] What is needed is a principle-based approach that will provide a conceptual framework within which consistency and cohesion can be achieved.

To address the financial-reporting excesses, major fundamental reform is now under way. The most important reform will be independent regulation of public accounting by the now independently funded oversight body (PCABO) reporting to the SEC. Effective independent oversight will include licensing and having disciplinary power.

While we might prefer standard setting to be done by the profession, public credibility now requires that this occur under the aegis of the independent oversight board. An unfortunate fact is that Arthur Andersen contributed more funds to congressional campaigns than Enron. (Perhaps this has given rise to the term "accounting industry," a phrase that grates on attuned sensibilities—it should be "the accounting *profession*.")

In any event, the "industry" has acquired so much political clout that true reform will have to be market-driven, rather than legislated. Fortunately, there are signs that this is now under way. For example, a number of major U.S. companies have voluntarily begun expensing stock options and have moved formerly off-balance-sheet debt to their balance sheets.

Against this backdrop, what is the role that internal audit should play? This book contends that it should be *an enhanced arm of corporate governance* rather than a group of second-string public accountants. We should not substitute increased internal audit activity directly for that which is required for the independent attest function expected from our CPA brethren. We can, however, add an important dimension that CPAs may not be as equipped to provide: *information-technology-driven continuous monitoring and forensic auditing focused on the fiduciary activity of management and potential conflict of interest, broad operating issues, and discretionary top-level accounting.*

Examples of these procedures include audit analyses of such things as:

- Off-balance sheet entities
- Discretionary reserves in general, and in particular, period-end, top-level journal entries to these accounts
- Related-party transactions
- Revenue-recognition issues such as questionable or unusual patterns at period-ends

- Increased interim disclosures now required by Sarbanes-Oxley
- Quality of earnings analyses: the aggressiveness and applicability of accounting policies and estimates
- Conflicts of interest and perquisites
- Insider trading activity and disclosures
- Accuracy and completeness of reports to the Audit Committee, which now must include all instances of management fraud, whether material or not

Note that the Sarbanes-Oxley Act requirement for management certification of financial reporting is now that the financials "fairly present," which is an arguably higher standard than just being in accordance GAAP. Moreover, the increased quarterly disclosures now required by Sarbanes-Oxley will virtually necessitate high-level real-time monitoring of the control structure. Certainly, an internal audit team is in the best position to perform the lion's share of this, presumably on an integrated or coordinated basis with the external auditors.

To be effective, our focus has to be on management controls and corporate governance at the top of our organizations, working closely with the audit committee. By markedly increasing information-technology-driven continuous monitoring to identify key indicators in real time, we can also provide a heightened awareness of management corruption, which primarily consists of conflicts of interest.

As commented on earlier, effective continuous monitoring requires substantial computing resources. The justification for such resources is twofold: the Sarbanes-Oxley requirements, of course, and effective deterrence of operating-management fraud, the largest single area of fraud loss.

Symptoms

Here are some symptoms of financial-reporting fraud:

- Substantial off-the-book entities (*special-purpose entities,* or SPEs) or transactions with related parties, particularly when inadequately disclosed.
- Unsupported journal entries around period-ends that have the effect of increasing P&L, particularly when the effect of such entries is to bring reported income in line with forecasts.

- Substantial discretionary reserves available for managing earnings, particularly when these are susceptible to subjective estimations and when such reserves fluctuate wildly.

- Journal entries involving discretionary reserves or having major P&L impacts that are made at the top, without meaningful support or explanation.

- Creative customer financing.

- Channel stuffing—bill-and-hold arrangements lacking the economic substance of sales.

- Reciprocal sales or swaps designed to inflate revenue.

- Related to the preceding symptom: incremental abuses of materiality (i.e., a "little bit here, a little bit there—it's not material"), which, in the aggregate, may indeed be material, particularly when used for creation of discretionary reserve cushions.

- Major restructuring charges that have the effect of sweeping understated expenses of prior periods under the carpet via nonoperating, nonrecurring charges.

- Via acquisition accounting, excessive write-offs of in-process R&D, thereby creating operating P&L cushions.

- Nonrecurring transactions affecting earnings that seem to pop up near the end of the period with something approaching regularity.

- Aggressive earnings targets that are always met exactly.

- Growth in revenue and income without commensurate increases in cash from operations.

- Volatile reported operating margins.

- Conversely, consistent margins that do not correlate with expanding results from operations.

- Earnings trends that are out of step with the company's industry peers or with what would be expected from external market conditions.

- Unrealistic future growth expectations due at least partly to growth resulting from unsustainable exogenous events (e.g., Y2K activity).

- A consistent pattern of growth inexplicably surpassing that of peer group(s), coupled with an excessive price-earnings (P/E) ratio.

- Aggressive accounting practices bordering on the inappropriate.
- Changes in accounting principles to a more favorable (for earnings) basis, particularly if not adequately disclosed.
- Operating management's dictation of inappropriate (or at least questionable) accounting principles and/or preoccupation with significant estimates, coupled with overly compliant accounting personnel.
- Intentional misstatements such as those resulting from "estimates" of items that are amenable to precise measurement.
- An unnecessarily complex organizational structure with a multiplicity of unusual legal entities with no underlying apparent business justification.
- Related to the preceding symptom: numerous or significant legal entities and/or bank accounts in tax-haven locations without any apparent underlying business justification.
- A lack of clear managerial accountability and lines of responsibility and authority.
- An absence of defined ethical standards, such as codes of conduct.
- Extreme and adverse consequences of significant pending matters, such as an acquisition or a merger, if unfavorable operating results were to be reported.
- A questionable ability to meet debt repayment obligations, particularly when controlling management may have personally guaranteed such obligations.
- The flip side of the preceding symptom: a significant contingent reward available to controlling management if the entity hits certain aggressive financial targets.
- A lack of transparency of financial statements and/or overly complex disclosures.
- A corporate culture of greed, coupled with extreme pressure to "make the numbers," frequently under the guise of a culture of performance.
- Open and tolerated conflicts of interest.
- Lack of financial literacy and/or independence on the audit committee.
- A disproportionate number of insiders on the board, coupled with a dominant CEO.

- Imperial CEO syndrome (see the preceding symptom): an exorbitant salary, coupled with an entitlement mentality, lavish perks, and excessive stock options.

- Imperial CEO syndrome may be accompanied by a dispensation of largesse to board members that creates at least the appearance of a lack of independence. This may take the form of significant contributions to affiliated charities, finders-fee bonuses, a significant level of business to related parties, or the like.

- A disproportionate amount of options outstanding and an overreliance on options as part of the compensation package(s).

- A large number of options scheduled to expire in the near future, particularly when such options are "out of the money."

- Insider selling, particularly when not disclosed—that is, formerly, when a "loan" was taken out from the company, stock sales could be used to repay the loan without having to be reported as insider sales.

- Abrupt, unexplained departures of key members of the management team.

- A business model that may have been based on faulty premises and may no longer be congruent with the external environment.

- An outsourced or ineffective internal audit department.

- Excessive nonaudit fees to the external audit firm.

- Excessive rotation of external auditors.

- Tone-at-the-top issues, such as prior securities law violations, nepotism, or heavy insider trading.

- Operating setbacks that would jeopardize available financing.

- Operating setbacks that would jeopardize covenants and result in severe unfavorable consequences.

Examples

In the late 1990s and early 2000s, revenue recognition had become the fraudulent financial-reporting technique of choice for those senior managers looking to provide the illusion of growth. This section provides three examples of how continuous monitoring could be used to detect various schemes designed to inflate reported revenue. (See Chapter 9 for additional examples.)

Period-End Sales Cutoffs.   Leaving the period open to increase recorded sales is an age-old practice. The symptom of this practice is extremely high recorded sales for the last few days of a period, frequently followed by unusually low sales for the early part of the following month. This would cause a peak-and-valley pattern because the company is, in effect, "robbing Paul to pay Peter" by moving sales from one period to another.

Recognize that this does not refer to the normal month-end increases that result from an energetic hustle to get things done. Rather, it concerns egregious increases that would be clearly implausible if anyone focused on the daily average sales totals. Consequently, the continuous-monitoring flag to look for is *average daily sales more than X standard deviations higher than normal, followed by a corresponding drop in the average daily sales for the first part of the subsequent period.*

This is based on the assumption that the underlying sales actually took place but were merely recorded in the wrong period. What sort of pattern, however, would accompany the situation in which the sales were totally fabricated—that is, there were no real underlying transactions? In such an instance, the typical continuous-monitoring flag would simply be *average daily sales egregiously above the norm* (*well more than X standard deviations*), *coupled with accounting entries from atypical sources—those other than the invoicing system—for example, general journal entries.*

Channel Stuffing.   Companies may inflate their revenue by offering incentives, such as abnormal discounts, right of return, or markedly extended terms, to their customers to take significant levels of extra deliveries above and beyond what would be expected. Typically, this occurs at the end of a period and amounts to "borrowing" sales from the next period. It usually entails an economic cost such as the aforementioned discounts and extended credit terms. If the deliveries really occurred, the practice may be considered poor business, but it typically is not fraudulent financial reporting.

If no delivery takes place, however, and the arrangement is a *bill and hold*, it may constitute an instance of *channel stuffing*. In this case, the economic substance of the transaction is such that a real sale has not occurred. Criteria such as the right of return or bearing the shipping cost of returns may indicate that ownership, with its attendant risks, has not really passed to a buyer.

In this case, the continuous-monitoring flags would be *markedly increased returns after the period-end; considerably extended, out-of-the-ordinary (for those particular customers) credit terms (e.g., 90 days if 30 were the norm); markedly increased discounts (also as compared to the norm for those customers); and other marked divergences from the norm for these types of transactions and customers.*

Swap Sales. Near the end of the stock market bubble, swaps or reciprocal sales were tactics used to create the impression of growth, which was valued at least as much as earnings in some industries. The classic examples occurred in the telecommunications industry, where excess capacity of Company A would be sold to Company B, while at the same time Company B would be selling similar excess capacity to Company A. Variations on this occurred in certain energy companies whereby simultaneous purchases and sales of exactly similar contracts at the same price furthered the illusion of growth.

Other variations on this theme included certain reciprocal sales between companies that were more of the nature of sham transactions to artificially boost reported revenue rather than actual, stand-alone transactions of economic substance.

The continuous-monitoring routines to detect these types of transactions involve identifying *simultaneous major sales and purchases to and from the same company(ies) that were recorded via journal entries or out of the ordinary billing/purchasing routines, particularly when such transactions were entered into at the same time, in similar amounts, and had other equal and offsetting aspects (same unusual credit terms, etc.).*

MONEY LAUNDERING/ILLEGAL PRACTICES

Concept

The basic concept of money laundering is that proceeds derived from an illegal activity are exchanged into usable, seemingly legitimate funds. Typically, the various regulations in place in the United States pertain to "financial institutions," as defined by the Bank Secrecy Act (BSA, Titles I and II of Public Law 91-508) and various related rules and regulations. In 2001, the Patriot Act markedly expanded the reporting requirements.

When money laundering occurs in a U.S. corporation, it's usually a rogue act, an unauthorized crime for the corporation. Typically, at least for the purpose of this book, the corporation is not the source of the illicit funds that are being laundered; rather, it is providing the means by which the funds are laundered, or it is "looking the other way" and accepting clearly questionable funds.

Fraud for the corporation is ultimately a zero-sum game: Although the individual employee "wins" in terms of receiving bonuses, raises, promotions based on enhanced operating results, and the like, eventually the company loses in terms of fines, penalties, and notoriety. Further, money-laundering services entered into knowingly by company management (or perhaps unknowingly but later brought to their attention) may render that management vulnerable to middle-management fraud, whereby a lower-level manager exploits this information for his or her own benefit.

Discussion

The normal flow of funds in money-laundering situations is circular, such as (considerably simplified):

- Illicitly earned funds are deposited by individual A in the U.S. account of a cutout (individual B), ostensibly in payment for some goods or services that are normally fictitious.

- The cutout would transfer the funds typically to an offshore bank account in a friendly, loosely regulated jurisdiction (e.g., the Caymans).

- The offshore bank account holder (individual B or a new individual C) then moves the funds back to individual A (this may or may not be in the United States).

- Individual A would then use these funds in an ostensibly legal fashion, such as the purchase of insurance, an investment instrument, or real estate. The chain could continue—this investment could quickly be used as collateral for a loan or, in the case of insurance, surrendered for the cash value.

The purpose is to move (or "wash") tainted funds until they reach an ostensibly legitimate, readily usable status.

A simpler chain of events may present itself—particularly if your company is not a financial institution—such that your company is not engaged as much in the movement of tainted funds as in the acceptance of them. (This would render the subsequent round-tripping unnecessary for individual A if he or she can just use the funds for an ostensibly legitimate purpose without fear that they will be traced.) This acceptance may be designed to enhance the marketability of a company's products (much like enhanced customer satisfaction) or to obtain an extra-high selling price.

One sales manager markedly increased his sales virtually overnight by accepting money-laundered funds. This is a more powerful ploy than extending credit to high-risk customers. Unfortunately for the company, because his superior knew and sanctioned his practice, the sales manager then effectively had license to steal. This was actually a chain reaction: The artificially increased sales afforded the owner the ability to sell his company to an acquirer, and then the former owner and the sales manager each engaged in their own major management fraud while in the employ of the new company.

When an internal auditor detects symptoms of possible money laundering or acceptance of questionable funds at his or her company, a whole array of concerns presents itself. The situation must be evaluated carefully in the context of the situational dynamics: Who benefits (and how), who knows (and when did they know), who is vulnerable because of their knowledge, and so forth. Legal responsibilities must be considered, particularly if the company is a financial institution as defined by the BSA or if the transactions would now qualify under the broadened criteria of the Patriot Act.

Under the Patriot Act, innocent nonfinancial institutions can now be affected by making deposits to their accounts of suspicious funds such as third-party money orders, cashier's checks, or wire transfers. Banks are now responsible for monitoring these deposits and, if they are deemed suspicious, reporting them via a Suspicious Activities Report (SAR). And, under the agency rule, the innocent (but perhaps foolhardy) nonfinancial institution can be prosecuted if the third-party payment it accepted turned out to be connected with money-laundering activity.

If the preceding is not enough, as a practical matter, consider the possibility that such license to steal might erupt elsewhere in the company if it closes its eyes to fraud in favor of the company by accepting money-laundered proceeds.

Symptoms

The following symptoms are far from all-inclusive; they are intended merely to serve as examples of the types of fund movements that might be encountered.

- A pattern of unusually large currency transactions to purchase negotiable instruments or initiate funds transfers, particularly if these transactions fall consistently just below the $10,000 threshold, and even more notably if they result in multiple checks written on the same day to the same payee. (See also the next symptom, "splitting.")

- Artificial splitting of currency transaction amounts in an apparent attempt to keep below the $10,000 threshold—for example, payment of a $25,000 receivable via transfers of $9,000, $8,000, and $8,000 on the same day.

- Large single payments from an international source, particularly one whose identity is obscured.

- Purchases or payments significantly above market value.

- Excessive incidence of cash currency transactions when this is not characteristic for these types of transactions.

- Payments from seemingly unrelated third-party payers or payments that obscure the identity of the payer, such as cashier's checks.

- Checks written without the payee line being filled in. On inspection, it is apparent that the payee was added subsequently.

- Evidence of shell companies.

- A pattern of implausibly early redemption of investments and transfer of proceeds to seemingly unconnected third parties.

- Purchases of significant cash investments that are quickly used as collateral for major loans.

CASE STUDY

STEROIDS FOR SALES (MONEY LAUNDERING)

XYZ Company has employed a growth-by-acquisition strategy fairly successfully. XYZ is a large multinational organization dealing globally in apparel and related manufacturing. While performing due diligence on a recently proposed acquisition, XYZ's internal auditors found suspicious activity prior to the acquisition.

This particular acquisition had been under discussion for over a year prior to establishing a letter of understanding. The initial projections indicated international annual sales in Asia of approximately $28 million, out of total annual sales of $61 million. As the auditors were eventually to discover, the initial pro forma statements were largely a fabrication. The company, Foundation Garments Inc., was actually limping along with relatively low-margin annualized international sales of approximately $8 million at that time. The steroids for the undernourished sales were about to arrive, however.

Shortly after the acquisition discussions began, a new manager of international sales for Foundation Garments, a Japanese national, had been hired. Sales soon escalated—so much so that they reached the annualized $28 million level only nine months after the new international sales manager's arrival. Based in large part on the suddenly robust Asian sales, the proposed acquisition moved forward.

At XYZ, the internal audit function gets involved in verification aspects of due diligence if any one of three conditions is met: The acquisition has problematic business measurement issues, there is a higher-than-average risk of sensitive payments, or the financial statements of the target company have not been certified by an external auditor that XYZ regards as reliable. In this case, Audit Manager John Vlasnik joked, "It looks like all of the above."

The level of international sales was identified as a key business issue. When the "too good to be true" pattern of explosive growth was encountered, the auditors knew what to look for.

The audit team performed standard substantive audit procedures such as confirmations and examining support to verify that the sales actually occurred. In addition, they obtained D&Bs on the customers and were struck by the curious nature of some of the major customers. They also noted that the major customers all seemed to have initiated their buying activities shortly after the new international sales manager arrived on the scene.

As a result, they obtained microfilm records from the bank of the actual composition of receipts that had been deposited to the Foundation Garments bank account. They found the following:

- Large cash currency amounts
- Payments from seemingly unrelated third-party payees
- Checks written for which the payee appeared to have been added subsequently
- Certain remittances that were composed of multiple money orders

The secret to the explosive growth in sales appeared to be easy acceptance of highly questionable proceeds—in other words, money laundering. The pattern was sales to Asian companies with payment effected in the United States by dubious funds.

Based on this information, XYZ Company's senior management dropped all plans to acquire Foundation Garments.

CASE STUDY

THE INDIVIDUAL IS NOT THE COMPANY

In "The Disappearing Sales" case study on commercial bribery later in this chapter, the audit team identifies streams of payments to three "consultants" that were actually bribes to obtain high-margin sales.

Background

The true nature of one series of payments became readily identifiable:

- These payments were $7,000 per month, for approximately two years, to a company called Eve Industries.
- For two years prior to this, the same $7,000 monthly amounts were recorded in the general ledger with a different payee, but *the mailing address was the same as that for Eve Industries.*
- The address was determined to be the home address of "John Adams," *who was the president of the largest customer, Quincy Industries.*

continued

Based on this information, and evidence of two similar streams of payments to individuals who turned out to be the decision makers at the other major customers, it was clear that commercial bribes had been used to obtain a significant level of sales that, absent such bribes, was not sustainable.

Follow-up

While using the audit software ACL to analyze the names and addresses of the disbursement files, the audit team discovered additional recurring payments to John Adams's home address. These were less frequent (say, every three months) and for odd amounts (such as $174,117)—and they were considerably larger.

By tracing the accounting entries, it was quickly determined that these represented returns of overpayments made by Adams's company, Quincy Industries. The auditors immediately recognized the issue: These payments had been received from Quincy Industries, the company, but were returned to Adams, the individual.

Audit Supervisor Dannelle Wilson suspected that these laundering-type payments were for the purpose of tax evasion. Her assumption was based on the premise that Adams was the sole owner of Quincy Industries, which she had been told, and which the pattern of commercial bribery seemed to support. However, as an experienced auditor, she knew that she had to validate this hypothesis—she also knew that surprises were frequent.

Working with Corporate Security, Dannelle set out to determine the facts relative to the ownership of Quincy Industries. She discovered the following:

- At the beginning of the period, Adams was not even the majority owner. Rather, for most of the period, he had 25 percent ownership, with an absentee owner, a Canadian, having 75 percent interest. During this period, it appeared that Adams was defrauding his majority owner (with the assistance of XYZ Company) via the transfers, in addition to the commercial bribery.

- About two years ago, Adams's company had itself been acquired. Consequently, although Adams remained the president, he was defrauding the new owners.

Dannelle determined that, over a four-year period, Adams had moved $2,878,117 from Quincy Industries to XYZ Company, which in turn served as a conduit and moved the funds back to Adams, but to his personal address rather than to the initiating company address. This was in addition to the commercial bribes of $336,000.

XYZ Company notified the appropriate authorities and affected parties, and the wheels of justice began to turn.

INTERNATIONAL ARENA

Concept

This topic could form a separate book, but here we will just provide a brief discussion. In the businesses that the author's various companies have been engaged in internationally, direct encounters with international corruption for the organization have been mainly in the areas of bribery and tax evasion. These two dimensions reflect, first, the generally different standards and rules for international business competition that our competitors play by and, second, off-the-books cash transactions as a pervasive way of doing business, as well as a method of tax evasion.

The Foreign Corrupt Practices Act (FCPA) of 1977, designed to eliminate bribes by U.S. companies to foreign officials, had one unintended effect: the creation of legalistic devices to circumvent the presumed limitations. This type of legalism is what Chapter 3 meant when it referred to ". . . convoluted structures . . . devised to accomplish business objectives of questionable legality."

In May 2002, Transparency International came out with its periodic survey on the propensity of companies to pay bribes: Bribe Payers Index 2002.[4] U.S. companies were tied with Japan for number eight. Companies from the following countries ranked ahead of the United States in their willingness to indulge in baksheesh: Russia, China, Taiwan, South Korea, Italy, Malaysia, and Hong Kong. Clearly, capitalism has triumphed over Marxism.

The risk that payment of foreign bribes poses to U.S. companies is twofold: (1) the danger of a clear-cut violation of the FCPA with the attendant penalties and (2) the effect of fraud *for* the organization on the propensity for fraud *against* the organization, which is potentially more significant from the standpoint of loss.

As for off-the-books cash transactions, primarily as a means of tax evasion, a prominent South American economist contends that the underground economy is larger and more robust than the aboveground economy in many lesser-developed countries (LDCs). In South America and the south of Europe, unrecorded sales (*black sales*), which are usually effected via cash, are common. Just as payment of bribes exposes the organization to leveraged fraud against the company, so do pervasive black sales open the door for such practices as opportunistic management abuse and money laundering.

Discussion

Anyone who believes that the Foreign Corrupt Practices Act of 1977 eliminated bribes by U.S. companies to foreign officials may still believe in Santa Claus (or at least the Easter Bunny). "We're number eight" is not a rallying cry that is likely to reflect favorably either on collegiate athletic prowess or national business ethics. However, a bit of context is in order. Before we get too judgmental, we should recognize that much of the world regards our standards as unrealistic (and hypocritical).

A major international construction company has stated publicly that there are over 70 countries in the world where they cannot compete without paying bribes. Their solution has been to put some legal distance between themselves and the bribe payers, such as sales agents or consultants. The author is aware of one major European multinational company whose general auditor allegedly administered the off-the-books slush funds used for paying governmental officials, including some in other European countries.

Transparency International reports that the industries in which bribes are most expected in the international arena are public works/construction, arms and defense, and oil and gas.[5] U.S. companies are major players in these industries. Clearly, for our companies to compete in these areas (and be assured, they are going to), they will have to lubricate the process. As the saying goes, where there's a will there's a way.

As noted, the effect of fraud for the organization on the propensity for fraud against the organization is potentially more significant from an actual loss standpoint. Chapter 3 cited "legalistic workarounds whereby convoluted structures or processes are devised to accomplish business objectives of questionable legality," such as circumvention of the bribery provisions of the

FCPA and dealings with certain prohibited countries. In the international arena, there are "hostage situations" whereby bribes are paid for the company and subsequently leveraged into fraud against the company via conflict-of-interest activities. Seymour Hersh's article in *The New Yorker*, "The Price of Oil,"[6] is a classic on this subject.

When it comes to the other area of fraud for the company in the international arena, contrary to popular belief, soccer is not the most popular sport in the south of Europe—tax evasion is. Just as the payment of bribes exposes the organization to leveraged fraud against the company, so do pervasive unrecorded sales.

The circumvention of tax regulations typically starts with unrecorded sales that are usually made in cash. In South America and the south of Europe, these unrecorded cash sales (black sales) are relatively common. In fact, the extent of the underground economy in Europe surfaced as a potential major obstacle to the introduction of the euro currency. One company elected to cancel a recent promising acquisition in a major South American country because it became clear that they would not be able to compete if they eliminated off-the-books cash transactions.

Symptoms

Not surprisingly, the symptoms of bribery in the international arena are very similar to those of commercial bribery in general. For additional symptoms, see "Commercial Bribery," later in this chapter.

- Arrangements whereby the recipients of commissions or consulting contracts are not personally identifiable, when the services provided are ill defined (or worse, linked too specifically to a quid pro quo), or when the payments appear to be disproportionate to the value provided. Bribes to obtain contracts (e.g., public works or arms sales) are typically large, up-front, nonrecurring payments, whereas "doing business" types of bribes are typically smaller and recurring.

- Recurring payments to cash or to third parties other than the indicated payee: bribes (or funding of slush funds).

- Payments under contingency-type arrangements that are correlated with volumes that would appear to have no connection with the service allegedly being performed—for example, payments to a consultant for "market advice" that are so much per unit of sales. Such contingency arrangements may be quid-pro-quo bribery.

- Rebates paid to individuals rather than to companies, particularly when the individuals are not readily identifiable.

- Conspicuously overpaying for an inherently difficult-to-value asset, such as intellectual property, particularly when the ultimate recipient of the payments is difficult to ascertain. This may be a well-disguised bribe.

- A variation on the preceding symptom: substantially overpaying for an inherently worthless asset, particularly when the recipient of the payment has a direct or once-removed connection with a governmental official (for example, a brother).

The symptoms of unrecorded cash sales (black sales) typically involve some aspect of deviations from recorded accountability. Examples are:

- Inventory shortages—or an absence of physical inventories (or certain classes of inventory that are systematically excluded from physical inventories).

- Excessive delays in billings.

- Excessive cash sales (or an inordinately high incidence of cash currency in collections and deposits).

- Delivery receipts missing. In some countries, mainly in southern Europe, delivery receipts are official, statutory records.

- Inexplicable routings whereby certain deliveries are not handled by third-party logistics providers even though the physical location would call for such routing. In these cases, the delivery is handled in-house to ensure that the paperwork reflects the desired information.

- Differences between purchasers per delivery receipts/bills of lading and sales invoices.

- Inexplicable lapses in access/egress plant or warehouse security, evidenced by such occurrences as a log not being maintained of trucks entering a plant, or a pattern of customers having access to the plant with no recorded sales.

- A pattern of compressed margins for certain inventory items or customers.

THE TELLTALE DELIVERY RECEIPTS

Background

The company for which Audit Manager Jane McMahon works, EFG Co., has been engaged in an aggressive acquisition program for some years now. The standard procedure is for internal audit to perform due diligence on potentially problematic matters prior to the acquisition and to perform a postacquisition audit approximately one year after the acquisition has closed, to facilitate integration of the acquired entity.

About one and a half years ago, EFG made an acquisition designed to effect entry into a business area in which they had considerable experience in the United States but only limited experience in Europe. This was a food processing and distribution business called Pommes Frites, s'il Vous Plais; the location was the south of France. Because of the relatively higher risk associated with this unfamiliar environment, internal audit initiated a more thorough due-diligence review than otherwise might have been the case.

In the planning phase, McMahon provided some business context for the audit team. She explained that tax evasion is common in southern Europe, at least for family-held businesses of the type that they were looking at acquiring. In particular, she described the relatively common practice of black sales, which are cash transactions off the books. These are used to beat both the value-added tax (VAT) and corporate income tax authorities. She advised the audit team that it was probable that the target company engaged in such sales to some extent.

Due Diligence—Black Sales

During due diligence, the owner of the acquisition target, Jacques Richac, acknowledged confidentially that black sales had been practiced "at about the same level as everybody else." While these sales were all off the books, in some instances (basically, when they involved larger quantities and third-party truckers) they could be identified by warehouse delivery receipts, which are similar to bills of lading as used in the United States. Frequently, however, black sales involved relatively small quantities, and those were not readily identifiable from books and records.

During the due-diligence work, the lead auditor, Jonathan Ford,

continued

obtained a list of names and addresses of customers to whom black sales had purportedly been made. He saved this for subsequent use on the postacquisition integration audit.

The due diligence and the acquisition were concluded without any additional major problems. Although EFG Co. management was emphatic that the black sales should be discontinued, the prior managing director of Pommes Frites, Jacques Richac, was left in place to run the business after acquisition. He appeared capable, and it was generally felt that the black sales were actually just a normal aspect of business in France—a "way of life."

Postacquisition

EFG Co.'s practice is that the lead auditor who performs the due-diligence audit also leads the postacquisition audit. In the planning phase, Jonathan performed the normal in-depth financial analysis. In particular, he focused on gross margin analysis over a comparative three-year period that covered periods both before and after the acquisition. He also looked at the vendors from whom Pommes Frites was purchasing.

His initial analysis indicated that margins had narrowed from the pre- to the postacquisition period, which bothered him: If black sales had been eliminated, he would have expected an improvement in margins. Consequently, he compared the results of the regular physical inventories taken and, again, could not obtain any assurance that the black sales had been discontinued. Rather, the pattern of regular inventory shortages that had been pervasive prior to the acquisition appeared to have continued postacquisition and, in fact, had gotten worse.

Thus, on arriving in the field, Jonathan got out his list of customers that had previously engaged in black sales. Jonathan instructed staff auditor Casey Young to find out whether sales had been billed to these customers. Casey reported back that none had. This was not reassuring—Jonathan would have preferred to find billings to these customers rather than being left with the feeling that the sales could have been made but not billed.

Casey, however, knew where to look next. The guard office at the plant maintained a list of all trucks entering the plant, including all customers' trucks. Casey found that the trucks owned by companies that had previously been involved in black sales were regularly entering the plant. Recognizing that there were no recorded sales to these customers, he reported to Jonathan that indications were that the practice had not been stopped.

Jonathan had him perform one more step: Casey compared the addresses of the customers to the delivery receipts on file in the warehouse. He discovered that there were continuing truckload deliveries to those addresses. He then compared these to the billings and discovered most of these transactions had not been billed.

There were two distinctly different patterns, however. Most sales in the north and middle of France were unbilled. In the southern part of France, however, sales were to companies that were geographically relatively close, and these were delivered by Pommes Frites trucks. All of these were billed, but to a company called Jacques et Freres that had no apparent direct connection to Pommes Frites; moreover, the profit margin on these sales was a small fraction of the normal margin.

Two Separate Issues

At this point, representatives from the security and law departments joined the audit team in the field. Additional facts were discovered via interviews with the black (cash) sales customers in the north and middle of France. These customers had in fact been the recipients of the deliveries. As had been their practice before, they continued to pay in cash, only now they were instructed to remit to one company in the south. Not surprisingly, that company was Jacques et Freres.

It was clear that Jacques et Freres was functioning as a middleman: In the north, the transactions were black sales in violation of VAT regulations; in the south, the difference was that VAT regulations were technically satisfied, and the loss to Pommes Frites was considerably less.

Given the emerging pattern, Jonathan anticipated what would unfold next, and he was not surprised. Corporate security determined that the owner of Jacques et Freres was no other than Jacques Richac, the general manager of Pommes Frites.

Since a considerable majority of the transactions and lost profits related to sales in the north, the first issue to be addressed was the company's circumvention of French VAT regulations. EFG Co. had Pommes Frites self-report expeditiously. After the auditors accumulated the total of the black sales by the recipient company, and considering that the transgression was inadvertent on the part of Pommes Frites/EFG Co., severe penalties for the company were avoided.

continued

The second issue was obviously the misappropriated profits on the part of the middleman. Unfortunately, because of the particular facts and circumstances, EFG Co. ended up chalking this one up to experience rather than prosecuting Richac, who was, of course, terminated. Obviously, not all frauds are prosecuted, particularly those wherein the "home court" advantage is absent.

PRICE-FIXING/BID RIGGING

Concept

The essence of price-fixing for the organization is the circumvention of competitive market forces. The classic form is dividing market shares and/or coordinating prices among companies that should be competitive. Related to this is the practice of *complementary bidding*. Tactics could also include commercial bribery.

This criminal activity (that's right—the Sherman Antitrust Act of 1890 made this a criminal offense) involves practices that unreasonably deprive consumers of the market advantages ascribed to competition in free, open markets. The economic premise was that by price-fixing, bid rigging, or assigning customers, the competitive free-market forces are stymied, and the effective allocation of resources by the system is distorted. The primary effect would be unnaturally high prices.

Discussion

Historically, these practices have been fairly common in many industries, in part because government enforcement has blown hot and cold, depending on the ideology of the party in power (the antitrust division of the Justice Department has primary responsibility). As Rosoff, Pontell, and Tillman maintain in *Profit without Honor,* "The illegality of price fixing has not often deterred its practice. A study of 582 large American corporations concluded that 'violations of the nation's antitrust laws are common in a wide variety of industries.' "[7]

Basically, the symptoms are the effects that would theoretically be observable in the marketplace; however, this is somewhat complex and beyond the scope of this book. Suffice it to say, symptoms could include coordinated price movements, consistent and constant market shares, and a pattern of complementary bidding—anything that would indicate coordinated, anti-competitive behavior. The key word is *pattern*.

One example of pattern analysis is a basic computerized statistical test that has been used by federal and some state agencies in analyzing bidding patterns on road-building contracts since the early 1980s. This involves factors such as number of bidders, patterns of bidding among certain contractors (e.g., whether certain contractors never bid against certain others), whether some bidders consistently win in some geographic areas and never win in others, patterns of bid rotation, and routine splitting of awards by subcontracting. An additional factor could be related-party ownership—relatives who are officers in erstwhile competitors.

Another, perhaps readily observable, symptom is "footprints" evidencing contact with competitors. This symptom might be observed in expense reports, telephone logs, e-mail, or, theoretically, in a diary (if the perpetrator had a burning desire for self-incrimination). One event that lends itself well to contact among competitors is trade shows.

In addition to pattern analysis and review for potential related parties, internal audit efforts could include review of business process risk management and legal compliance efforts such as employee training, dissemination of a code of ethics, or an employee hot line.

Symptoms

Here are some symptoms of fraud involving price-fixing or bid rigging:

- Egregious price increases that stick. One reference cites an example of a price increase of 3000 percent.[8]

- On bidding of construction contracts, a pattern of taking turns being the low bidder, perhaps supplemented by apparent complementary competitive bids (i.e., those that are not serious attempts to win). Also look for a pattern of the last bid being the winner.

- A variation on the preceding symptom includes a pattern of subcontracts: a limited number of bidders taking turns as the winner, and the same companies working together as subcontractors over extended periods for the rotational winners.

- A pattern of consistent, seemingly coordinated price increases, particularly when these involve preannouncement. The classic example was in the airline industry, which allegedly signaled fare hikes in advance via their electronic databases.

- Consistent and constant market share over an extended time period. This may also follow geographic patterns.

- Tight control over the pricing authority of the sales force, such as situations wherein all prices have to be approved by centralized management.

- Evidence of contact with competitors. This symptom could be observed in expense reports, telephone logs, e-mail, or possibly in a diary.

- Illegal contact at trade association meetings, which afford the pretense (and thereby the cover) of sanctioned interaction among companies that would otherwise be competitors.

CASE STUDY

PRICE-FIXING DISCUSSION

Instead of case studies drawn from the author's experience, this section discusses two instances of price-fixing drawn from the public domain. The first is the prototypical case of price-fixing: the General Electric/Westinghouse price-fixing scandals of the 1950s. The second is one of the most bizarre occurrences in the annals of modern business: the Archer Daniels Midland (ADM) lysine price-fixing scandal that played out in virtual real time in the national financial press in the mid-1990s.

The Great Electrical Conspiracy

Before there was collusion, there was a fierce price war. General Electric (GE) had long dominated the market for heavy transformers; however, Westinghouse gained the first advantage by successfully entering this market. GE shot back by drastically cutting prices on transformers and other heavy electrical equipment.

The battle raged for some time and impaired the profitability of all involved. (The author grew up in one of the communities in which a major transformer plant was located. As a young teenager, I can remember hearing about the price wars.) After the effects on profits were recognized, cooler heads eventually prevailed, and the companies went from the ridiculous to the economic sublime (for them).

According to *Profit without Honor,* "Instead of submitting competitive sealed bids for lucrative government contracts, executives began holding secret meetings at which they would agree in advance on prices and divide up the contracts among their respective firms. . . . The companies had effectively formed an illegal cartel. . . . The scheme came unglued in 1959, when a communication miscue within the cartel resulted in the submission of identical, supposedly competitive bids to the federally controlled Tennessee Valley Authority. . . . The Justice Department examined TVA records and discovered 24 other instances of matching bids over a 3-year period. Some of these bids were figured down to one 1/100th of a cent. The investigation soon revealed that bid-rigging was by no means peculiar to the TVA. It had become an endemic way of life industry-wide."[9]

The total fines amounted to $2 million, which were substantial in the early 1960s, but which were in fact only a fraction of the illegal profits obtained through the bid rigging.

Lysine Price-Fixing

In this case, truth is much stranger than fiction. This bizarre tale involves a troubled government informer who had been on the fast track to become (perhaps) the next CEO of Archer Daniels Midland (ADM). The informer, Marc Whitacre, ended up as one of the defendants—and part of the evidence against him was a meeting that he had taped on behalf of the FBI. And this is before the really weird stuff.

The lysine price-fixing involved ADM and some Japanese companies in a scheme designed to support market prices by limiting production and allocating shares of the market. The players met in California at a hotel. The meeting was secretly videotaped by Whitacre: An agreement was established (and recorded on tape), and everyone left satisfied that the purpose had been accomplished.

Soon, however—perhaps because the agreement had not been documented in writing—confusion arose, and the parties needed to meet again. This time, they convened a trade association meeting for cover and met in a hotel. Again, Whitacre taped the meeting (room service was provided by the FBI).

continued

So far so good: The FBI eventually raided the ADM offices, and a price-fixing case was being developed. At this point, however, Whitacre called the *Wall Street Journal* and went public. He was, of course, fired by ADM. He then contacted other reporters and, eventually, *Fortune* magazine.

In August 1995, ADM released the story that Whitacre had embezzled and money-laundered a substantial amount of company funds, which was essentially correct. Whitacre first attempted a cover story (under-the-table bonuses) and then, unsuccessfully, suicide. Since Whitacre was now useless to the FBI, they struck a deal with the Japanese, who rolled over onto ADM. Whitacre and two other high-ranking ADM executives, including the CEO's son, were prosecuted and convicted.

It was eventually determined that Whitacre had been deceived by a fraudulent get-rich-quick appeal—to wire transfer funds to Nigeria—and then stole from ADM to recover. Then, for whatever reason, he con-cocted a story to the CIA about a Japanese saboteur, which brought in the FBI. At this point, Whitacre provided the FBI with information related to his employer's price-fixing scheme, and the rest is history.

COMMERCIAL BRIBERY

Concept

Bribery is traditionally thought of in the context of a quid-pro-quo arrange-ment whereby something of value is offered (the quid) to influence an offi-cial act (the quo). In the traditional, and somewhat limited, sense, the official act would be a decision or act by a governmental agent or employee in their official capacity. The term "commercial bribery" broadens the tradi-tional definition to include business as well as governmental decisions and actions.

Since this section discusses fraud for the organization, our focus is on the payment of bribes. Obviously, for every payer, there is a recipient; however, the recipient would be engaged in fraud against the organization. Typically, the recipient of a commercial bribe is engaged in some aspect of bid rigging or contracting fraud, which was discussed in Chapter 5 from the standpoint of management conflict-of-interest fraud against the organization.

Adopting the nomenclature of the ACFE reports, bribery of management personnel (broadly defined) is typically bid rigging; bribery of employees involves kickback schemes. The difference largely depends on the scope and amount of the influence purchased: the median loss from a bid-rigging scheme is $2 million; the median loss under a kickback scheme is $250,000.[10] Although kickback schemes were twice as frequent, bid-rigging schemes resulted in almost three times the total amount of losses.[11]

Discussion

Although bribes can be paid directly to the recipient, larger ones that would be more typical in management fraud are usually disguised. The easiest way to disguise them is to pay them off the books, out of slush funds established for that purpose. Another way many companies disguise them is to ascribe an erstwhile business purpose to the payments. The classic example has been to call them payments for consulting services.

There are certain fuzzy areas for which accountability for receipt of goods or services is difficult to establish, measure, or value. Examples of these are:

- Intangible services for which the performance or receipt may be difficult to track, such as consulting services, certain maintenance services, and advertising.

- Areas inherently difficult to value such as real estate, some subcontracts, and consulting services (again).

These fuzzy areas may be conducive to commercial bribery (classically, consulting services), or they may be the means to carry out larger, more complex frauds (e.g., real estate and related-party fraud).

Historically, the use of consultants—either as direct recipients of influencing payments in visible quid-pro-quo scenarios or, more commonly, as conduits to the ultimate recipients—was the method of choice for many companies, particularly in the international arena. In the 1970s, the disclosure of rampant bribery in the international arena, particularly for defense and armament sales to foreign governments, and illegal campaign contributions domestically led to the Foreign Corrupt Practices Act of 1977.

It is also worthwhile to note briefly the concept of *criminogenic industries*. These are industries in which the traditional norm is an expectation of fraudulent behavior ("It's a way of life"). Typically, this would be fraud *for* the company, which, as we've seen, usually becomes fraud *against* the company. Such fraud typically involves commercial bribery or bid rigging.

In the United States, although some formerly borderline criminogenic industries now have cleaned up their acts, historical examples include hazardous waste and garbage disposal, certain construction industries, and casinos. In the international arena, Transparency International lists the top three industries for bribery as public works/construction, arms/defense, and oil and gas.[12]

Obviously, wherever and however it occurs, the practice of management-condoned commercial bribery opens the door for a progression from fraud for the company to fraud for the individual *against* the company. Perhaps equally important, when uneconomical practices are used to support slush funds, the visible disregard for good practice leads to an absence of performance accountability and discipline.

From an audit/investigative standpoint, off-the-books bribery schemes are the most difficult to detect. For that reason, an effective audit dynamic is to focus on the funding, emphasizing the ultimate accountability for payments, in terms of controls, support, and commensurate value received. For payments that are on the books, the most important aspect is determining the identity of the ultimate recipient(s).

Symptoms

Here are some symptoms of fraud involving commercial bribery:

- Consulting payments that are linked to sales volumes or that are excessive for the services provided or for which there's no evidence as to what is provided. These can cover a multitude: bribes, illegal payments such as political contributions, or simple fraud for personal benefit.

- A continuing pattern of implausible, excessive, unsupported, under-explained expense report reimbursements. Possible reimbursement of influence payments (commercial bribery: reimbursement of kickbacks paid), or support of a slush fund.

- Somewhat similar to the preceding symptom, a pattern of sizable undersupported payments to consultants.

- Again similar to the preceding symptom, apparent advances expensed directly, rather than establishing recorded accountability. Possible reimbursement of influence payments or kickbacks, or support of a slush fund.

- Movement of funds in and out such that the organization serves as a gratuitous conduit, particularly when the recipient is difficult to identify. This can involve support of slush funds or payment of bribes; alternatively, this might be fraud against the organization by means of other fraudulent disbursements.

- Recurring payments to cash or to third parties other than the indicated payee. Again, this may involve support of slush funds or payment of bribes, or, alternatively, fraud against the organization by an other fraudulent disbursement method.

- Payments under contingency-type arrangements that are correlated with volumes that would appear to have no connection with the service allegedly being performed—for example, payments to a consultant for market advice that are so much per unit of sales. Such contingency arrangements may be quid-pro-quo bribery.

- Rebates paid to individuals rather than to companies.

- Conspicuously uneconomical practices, particularly when conducted openly. After first eliminating management stupidity and/or incompetence as reasons for the unsound activity, next rule out basic conflict of interest. Focus on how visible the practice would be to the management chain of command, and if it is conspicuous and open (and if no action occurs to stop it after initial recognition), consider the possibility of slush fund support.

- Conspicuously overpaying for an inherently difficult-to-value asset, such as intellectual property, particularly when the ultimate recipient of the payments is difficult to ascertain. Put bluntly, this may be a well-disguised bribe.

- Doing business over time with a company whose sole—or at least primary—rationale is to do business with your company. Look to the economic substance of the relationship.

- A pattern of substantial payments to one company for essentially unverifiable services, particularly when these payments reflect substantial budget overruns.

- A variation on the preceding symptom whereby numerous payments are made to apparently different payees who really are the same business entity, in an attempt to obscure the total payments to that payee, for example, payments for consulting or other intangible services. This is potential management or procurement relationship fraud, or it may also be payment of a bribe or the creation of a slush fund.

- A pattern of substantially uneconomical practices at multiple locations controlled by one manager—for example, substantial excess cash balances at all international locations or freight abuses involving one carrier at multiple locations. The underlying concept is inexplicable happenings at multiple locations with a common management denominator.

- Uncharacteristic treatment of one company, such as early payment to one vendor when all others are paid in 45 days.

CASE STUDY

COMMERCIAL BRIBERY—THE DISAPPEARING SALES

Background—Disappearing Sales

XYZ Company manufactures sophisticated security systems for a variety of industries and applications, including certain governmental entities. The key element is a sensitive photoelectronic cell that detects motion. XYZ has linked this to various IT applications that provide a wide range of flexibility and adaptability for the basic process.

One small division that sells a relatively specialized version domestically to nongovernmental entities is called Certified Internal Secure Applications (CISA). This division had been extremely successful over an extended period until about one year ago, when sales fell off precipitously. At that time, the division general manager suddenly left the company. Her successor had been in place for about 10 months and had requested an internal audit.

The new general manager was unhappy with the performance of the division, in part because of the intractability of sales, which showed no signs of an imminent return to the prior levels. He had asked the audit team to focus on opportunities for business improvements.

In the planning phase, Audit Supervisor Dannelle Wilson quickly identified one obvious problem: Sales to the former three largest customers had virtually evaporated shortly before the departure of the former general manager. These three customers—Quincy Industries, Bombay Products, and California Dreaming—had accounted for approximately 40 percent of the total sales and approximately 55 percent of the gross profits.

Explanation

When asked about the disappearing sales, the sales manager, who had been in place for some time, contended that XYZ Company had recently lost its technological advantage and now wasn't able to sell effectively to these accounts. The sales reps assigned to these accounts, however, had a different version. They informed Dannelle that they had been told by the purchasing agents at all three companies, "Your company's prices are not even close to being competitive. Previously, we were instructed by our management to buy from you—but that's not the case anymore."

Dannelle looked at the historical margins on the sales to these accounts prior to the recent decline, and it was apparent that the customers' buyers were correct: The three accounts were the only purchasers of a very specialized product. Furthermore, it was clear that the sales prices had always been substantially above those of the prevailing market. Still more bad news: Due to existing supply contracts, there was no way that XYZ Company could profitably sell this particular product at the prevailing market prices.

Dannelle had considerable experience and recognized the emerging outline of what may have actually happened. Consequently, the audit team began an in-depth review to determine whether questionable payments of an influencing nature had been made at the direction of the former general manager.

Identification of One Payee

As an experienced auditor, Dannelle started with the general ledger account consulting services. Not surprisingly, three series of repetitive payments were apparent.

continued

The true nature of one series of payments became fairly readily identifiable:

- These payments, which stopped just before the departure of the former general manager, were $7,000 per month and extended back for approximately two years. The payee was a company called Eve Industries.

- For the two-year period prior to that (counting backward, years three and four prior to the departure of the previous general manager), the same $7,000 monthly amounts were recorded in the general ledger, but the payee was different. *The mailing address, however, was the same as that used for Eve Industries.*

- By reference to a Haines Directory (a reference source commonly known as a *crisscross*), the address was determined to be the home address of a "John Adams." One of the D&Bs obtained for the three major accounts that had been lost indicated that *John Adams was the president of Quincy Industries, the larger of the two customers.*

One of the other streams of payments was not quite as easily identifiable, and one was extremely easy.

Identification of the Easy Payee

One stream of payments, to Marketing Metrics Associates, was less frequent and quite irregular in amounts. These payments appeared to Dannelle to be on a three-month cycle. By working with the crisscross, she determined that the payments were being mailed to the home address of a Martin Singh. The next step was easy. She had already obtained D&Bs for the three customers whose sales had disappeared. Sure enough, Singh was the general manager of California Dreaming.

When Staff Auditor Casey Young found the supporting agreement for the payments, the solution was simple. The quarterly payments to Marketing Metrics for "marketing consulting services" were based on a consulting agreement; however, the basis for the quarterly amount was the sales to California Dreaming for the preceding quarter.

Casey was not very experienced, but he recognized a bribe when he saw one. He complained to Dannelle, "That was too easy."

Identification of the Difficult Payee

For the last four years prior to the sales drop-off, a monthly amount of $6,200 had been paid to various companies and recorded as "consulting services." Each year, however, the name of the company being paid was different.

The first breakthrough actually came from the correspondence file maintained in the Sales Department for one of the major customers. In this file, Casey found the name of an individual who had the title "Director of Technical Processes, Research and Development" for Bombay Products. In discussion with the sales rep who currently dealt with that account, Casey determined that *the functional responsibility of this individual was "technical gatekeeper"—that is, he qualified all technological products for purchase by Bombay Products.*

Casey obtained this person's home address from the phone book and compared it to the accounts payable name and address files for the series of $6,200 payments to determine a chain of connections:

- Four years ago, the address used for the payments to the company for that year was the same as the technical director's address. Although a different company name was used for the payments the following year, the address was still the same.

- Then, two years ago, a different company name was used, along with a post office box. The supporting documents, however, were monthly invoices in the name of the new company—but these still carried the same street address as the preceding payments.

In the last year prior to the drop-off in sales, there was no immediately obvious connection to the technical director of Bombay Products. Casey was resourceful; he called the technical director's listed home phone number and posed as an office supply salesman. He discovered that the company whose name was used for the series of payments in the final year was domiciled at the same address and phone number as the technical director (he did, however, report to Dannelle that he had not been able to sell them any office supplies). *Clearly, the ultimate recipient of all of these payments over the four-year period was the decision maker for Bombay Products.*

Resolution

The questionable nature of the consulting payments and the reason for the disappearing sales were quite clear. By pursuing the accounts payable documentation, the auditors determined that all of the ques-

continued

tionable payments were generated by check requests prepared and approved by the former general manager. Moreover, the administrative assistant reported that these payments had been "walked through,"—in other words, paid on an expedited basis—and the checks returned to the former general manager, who would usually hand-deliver them.

Obviously, XYZ Company had inadvertently been involved in a commercial bribery scheme. Clearly, the company had no alternative other than to self-report. Given that they self-reported and cooperated, the authorities were not punitive. Such was not the case for the former general manager and her "consultants."

The former general manager and the recipients of the bribes—the president of Quincy Industries, the general manager of California Dreaming, and the technical director for Bombay Products—were prosecuted by the local authorities. All were convicted, and appropriate restitution to the affected companies was arranged: XYZ's general manager returned her last four years' bonuses and profit sharing to the company, and the other companies' trust violators returned the amounts of the bribes to XYZ and treble damages to their respective companies.

Moreover, although the particular product that Quincy Industries, California Dreaming, and Bombay Products had been buying from XYZ was no longer competitive, all of these companies stepped up their purchases of other products from XYZ.

Postscript

In reviewing the payments to Eve Industries/John Adams, a related anomaly was noted. This was followed up separately and became a more telling smoking gun. See the case study "The Individual Is Not the Company," earlier in this chapter.

CHAPTER 8

Methodology: Detection/Investigation

DIFFERENCES—MANAGEMENT VERSUS EMPLOYEE ACCOUNTING-CYCLE-TYPE FRAUD DETECTION/INVESTIGATION

Given the differences between major management fraud and financial-reporting/accounting-cycle fraud, you would expect that management fraud would be detected and investigated somewhat differently. Much of the focus of this discussion of detecting and investigating management fraud, however, may also be applicable to lower-level fraud—for example, the cubbyholes in the structure for recorded accountability that permit fraudulent debits to be hidden.

It is important to acknowledge that there is a major difference between recognition and detection and the subsequent investigation. One company expects that *all* of the auditors are able to recognize the red flags of major management fraud; only *some,* however, will be able to carry the initial phase of detection through to the point of determining the probability of actual fraud.

Thereafter, when this company moves into the investigative phase, certain aspects, such as the forensic accumulation of evidence in a legal form, will involve specialized skills that would normally reside outside the internal audit department. That said, in dealing with the relevant concepts and principles of fraud and recognition and detection/investigation, it is useful to group these methodologies together rather than deal with them separately.

RECOGNITION/DETECTION

There is no clear line of demarcation between recognition and detection. A convenient (but oversimplified) way to view the process is as a continuum, with recognition as the first step in the recognition, detection, and investigation fraud chain. Recognition is the proverbial light bulb that goes off as the auditor becomes aware of the *possibility of fraud* and *how it may have occurred.* Detection is the next step: determining the *probability of fraud.*

Optimally, recognition would occur during the planning phase of an audit assignment. Whenever it occurs, earlier is better than later, so be sure to consider the relevant risk factors in your planning stage—but be equally sure to keep yourself open to the possibilities of fraud recognition as you conduct your audit. The following tips would be most useful during the earliest stages of the audit:

- Perform financial analyses, particularly gross profit analyses, for extended periods—for at least three years. The reason for a three-year perspective is simply that trends and/or sore-thumb anomalies are not observable by a simple two-year comparison. A two-year pattern does not constitute a trend.

- Use tools and techniques such as CAAT/ACL and joining files extensively, focusing on patterns and anomalies. Just as "location, location, location" is the key to real estate, *patterns, patterns, patterns* are central to fraud recognition and detection, and effective pattern recognition is enhanced by imaginative CAATs. In particular, joining files creates a relational database that can provide a view of patterns that is not otherwise visible.

- Use Benford's Law more for high-level indications of broad possibilities. Benford's will point you in the direction of possible artificial (i.e., human) intervention in data files that would indicate the possibility of fraudulent transactions, but it won't usually lead you to the particular transactions directly. A more useful variation based on a similar principle is this: Look for even thousands of dollars, such as transactions ending in $000 when that would be an unusual amount to appear in records.

- Focus on the red flags—both common ones such as KPMG's and any symptoms similar to the red flags of management fraud cited in Chapter 4. There will be individual variations in these symptoms that are particular to your company and industry.

- In particular, the internal audit function can strengthen the due-diligence process by searching for questionable payments. Explicit verification of the identity of all consultants and/or commission agents and the nature of such services is invaluable. Similarly, for ongoing continuous monitoring of potentially sensitive payments (i.e., fraud for the organization), as well as monitoring opportunities for personal enrichment, this is a fertile area. One useful tactic for continuous monitoring is to combine this with wire transfer monitoring, building in the additional criterion of an unusually high approval level for the transaction.

- Remember that there will always be a story to explain away implausible lifestyle manifestations. Frequently, this story involves some aspect of an inheritance, because the lifestyle phenomenon often appears suddenly, seemingly out of nowhere. Remember that inheritances are normally verifiable.

- When a company is engaged in questionable practices, consider this to be a red flag indicating the potential for fraudulent personal gain. The existence of such gain becomes more likely due to the perpetrator's perceived sense of the diminished probability of prosecution. Fraud becomes easier for the perpetrator if a company is engaged in questionable practices. In particular, when artificial cutouts are established to create a once-removed layer between the ultimate business activity and the organization in order to continue activities that cannot legally be conducted directly by the organization, this creates a virtual carte-blanche opportunity for manipulation for personal gain.

- Keep in mind the holes in the P&L accountability and the lack of recorded accountability. The key to the longevity of fraud is the perpetrator's ability to avoid the P&L scrutiny, the accountability spotlight. Where is the black hole in your company's system of accountability? In particular, when you have identified such structural anomalies, use these for information-technology-driven continuous monitoring.

- While the holes in the P&L system of accountability are useful for recognizing fraud, the best way to commit fraud is to never record the transaction in the first place (e.g., by diversion of sales). This is why operating management corruption and conflict of interest are particular challenges for internal auditors. In this regard, remember Arthur Conan Doyle's "dog that didn't bark" from his Sherlock Holmes series relative to diverted revenue or profits that should be there but aren't.

- Accounting systems and controls for products that are out of the company's operational mainstream are usually weaker than the mainstream processes. When the unique weaknesses of these nonmainstream processes are superimposed on the normal general control weaknesses, the resulting total weakness may be greater than the sum of the individual parts, thus creating negative synergy.

- A company hot line can be invaluable for recognizing potential fraud. Keep in mind that the information will require filtering and interpretation because the caller will usually have only a single piece of the picture. The conventional wisdom is that information received via a hot line is valid and useful only about 10 percent of the time. Based on our experience, this is considerably understated but probably reflects the fact that the callers have only limited information. It is up to the investigator to fit that piece of information into the puzzle.

- A variation on hot lines that some companies have used to positive effect is an annual code-of-conduct affirmation. The code of conduct is distributed annually, and all employees are required to affirm that they have read and understood it, and, moreover, that they will abide by it. This is a fairly basic process and is just good practice. A recent positive spin on this practice is requiring employees to affirm that they have not seen nor are they aware of any violations of the code of conduct. This can also include requiring them to disclose the details of all violations of which they have knowledge. Given the effect of Sarbanes-Oxley on U.S. business, this ethical affirmation will likely become more prevalent. We strongly recommend it.

DETECTION/INVESTIGATION

Just as recognition typically precedes detection, detection precedes investigation. Recognition and detection are more intertwined, with no clear line of demarcation. Normally, investigation is a distinctly separate step in the fraud chain; however, certain areas do overlap. The following tips are useful in both phases of the fraud chain:

- Verify inventory (satisfy yourself that it's not significantly distorted) and bank reconciliations, and consider confirming receivables. Although this step is extremely basic, do not overlook it, particularly the inventory verification. This step is not concerned with the type of material inventory overstatement that rises to the level of fraudulent financial reporting; rather, it refers to the cushions that can be created by overstated inventory. These more modest overstatements would typically be used in conjunction with cubbyholes in the P&L structure that can be used to absorb the total fraudulent debit effect.

- Establish and use timelines, with particular emphasis on inflection points: What happened at that time to cause the change in question? Timelines are useful in analyzing purchase and sales volumes (see below) to flag the appearance of middleman companies. Use an extended period of at least three years. Note that a timeline can also be particularly useful for determining and demonstrating who was involved, when, and, by inference, how.

- Look at the *fraud life cycle* for changes over the extended time period during which the fraud took place. These changes will usually occur in response to fluctuating external circumstances. In an almost Darwinian sense, the process and mechanics of the fraud will evolve and change their shape. In particular, consider such changes in the context of the control structure and changes thereto.

- Pay particular attention to the process and mechanics of the fraud in its early stages because frequently the perpetrator will not have all the bugs worked out in the beginning. You might be able to pick up on something like an address that would be obscured later as the fraud grows larger and more complex.

- Typically, employee fraud starts relatively small and becomes larger over time as the perpetrator becomes more emboldened. Management fraud does not normally display this slow-starting characteristic to the same extent that employee fraud does; nevertheless this tendency may be present in certain instances of management fraud.

- Expect surprises in any complex fraudulent action. Nothing is ever entirely as it appears initially. In a complex fraudulent action of extended duration, the total loss is invariably bigger than it initially appears, and it often involves individuals other than the immediately obvious perpetrators. The potential for involvement further up the management chain is the reason IIA Practice Advisory 1210.A2-1 states: "Assess the probable level and the extent of complicity in the fraud within the organization. *This can be critical to ensuring that the internal auditor avoids providing information to or obtaining misleading information from persons who may be involved*"[1] [emphasis ours].

- Use volumes—typically, in descending order—of annual purchases and sales to identify middlemen. Middleman activity, which is the artificial interjection of an entity between your organization and the ultimate customer, is a strong red flag indicating fraudulent activity.

- Keep in mind the cockroach theory: Where one fraud exists, others are more probable. And, while they may or may not be related, they may share the same account coding, the dumping ground for fraudulent debits.

- The concept of a dumping ground for fraudulent debits is useful for a kind of reverse-engineering process: When you have discovered the account code or codes that provide the cubbyhole for hiding the debits related to a fraudulent activity, look for other charges to this account and trace them back. You may discover other instances of fraud that you had not been aware of.

- Behavior at either end of the aggression continuum—either overly aggressive or meekly submissive—can be indicative of having something to hide. Uncharacteristic behavior on the part of a fraud suspect can be even more significant.

- Determine the true identity of middleman companies. Use D&Bs, state records of incorporation, and the like, and be alert to identifying nominee owners rather than true owners. In real estate fraud, a pattern showing the same people as nominee owners can be indicative.

- Make yourself available to employees. They will know and volunteer more information than you realize—and you will find that they actually know more than *they* realize. For this to be successful, you have to provide a secure and confidential setting to facilitate candid discussion.

- Recognize the superiority of an external record (and information) over internal records. This external record might include the telephone book, incorporation records, post office boxes, or bills of lading bearing real shipping addresses. Use these extensively. Because fraud involves deception and many internal records are under the control of the perpetrator, you should perform a comparison between the internal and the external records to highlight significant differences.

- Talk to third parties. You will be surprised what they will tell you, even over the phone and without verifying your identity. Thus, you might wish to carefully prepare the way you phrase your request for information to avoid disclosing to the target that an investigation is under way.

- One missing file or document does not necessarily represent anything unusual (quite the contrary). A pervasive pattern of missing files or records, however, can be a bright red flag. The fraud suspect may make it difficult to locate files and documents in order to discourage investigative efforts. Do not be lazy or shoddy in your methods, but neither should you be paranoid.

- Comparing shipping records to billing records is a basic fraud investigation technique that is also useful in the United States for disclosing middleman companies and other billing scams. Although simple, it is particularly effective because invoices can be created for any address, but truckers need the actual delivery address for physical movement of goods. Consequently, the real delivery address is usually available on an unalterable document.

INVESTIGATION

After recognition and detection have determined the possibility and then the probability of fraud having been committed, investigation would normally be performed by those individuals with more specialized skills. Much of this investigation is what is frequently referred to as forensic, a substantial portion of which relates to paralegal preparation of the case for eventual entry into the legal system. This book does not focus on these more specialized skills; however, the following tips on procedure should be within the competency of a well-trained, experienced internal auditor:

- Coordinate your procedure with the security department, and be sure that each operates within its particular area of expertise. My future company refers to these two parties as "Mr. Inside" and "Mr. Outside," which reflects how the investigative work is divided. Basically, the security function focuses on external records, such as state incorporation records and arrest records, and agencies, while the internal audit function focuses on internal records. Interviews of company employees are conducted jointly.

- Coordinate your efforts with the legal department and other involved parties. Establish a protocol in the beginning for who is responsible for what. This is particularly important because the natural propensity for legal departments is to restrict the flow of information. On a complex fraud investigation, real-time communication to the entire—and frequently extended—team is imperative.

- Establish "attorney work product" privilege at the outset, while recognizing that it may not stand up. The key is to get it in place at the beginning of an investigation. The theory is that the investigation is being conducted at the request of, and under the control of, the legal department. Obviously, any reports emanating from such an investigation will be addressed to the legal department and will have a severely limited distribution. The internal audit department will have to control all aspects of the investigation that they think are necessary.

- Take time to get the lay of the land rather than jumping right in. Develop a feel for the outer perimeter of what you might be uncovering. An elaboration on this approach is assessing the potential for involvement further up the management chain before initiating the investigation.

- Hypotheses drive and direct the investigation, not the other way around. Do not, however, conclude too soon. Continually reevaluate your hypotheses as new information becomes available. This is the "five card stud" theory of investigation: Just as a skilled poker player knows that every time a new card is turned over the probabilities have to be recalculated, so does the skilled auditor recognize the fluid impact of new information.

- Be sure to look for *horizontal* connections as well as *vertical:* extend what's been learned in one area to other areas to ascertain the existence of related fraud. Be alert for cross-connects—the seemingly unrelated phenomena. This pertains particularly to management fraud involving individuals at or near the top of the organization or fraud in which there is a related fraud for the company.

- Use enforcement agencies smartly, while recognizing the potential conflict of different agendas. In particular, remember this: Enforcement agencies have subpoena power; you don't. However, you have expertise in white-collar crime and the concomittant resources; they usually don't. When you work together, you create synergy. Involve your security and legal departments in this process.

- Use company resources carefully and discreetly to obtain confidential information that might not be readily available otherwise. As an example, consider using your treasury department's bank sources to obtain certain information such as potential undisclosed ownership interests or signatories on third-party bank accounts. Be sure to consult your legal department first.

- Use other companies' internal audit departments to obtain information. As long as the information is not detrimental to their interest, they will usually be helpful. In one instance, we used such a source to determine that what was billed to us as tires (but without the required tax) was really a color TV. The relevant principle is that we all have an interest in ethical business practices.

- The fraud perpetrator will often keep a scratch-sheet type of record. Look for this. It is necessary for the mechanical conduct of certain types of fraud, such as lapping. This scratch-sheet record may also be saved in a PC's hard drive.

- Use the Norton Utility software to capture data that the perpetrator tried to delete from a PC. You are probably aware that the simple "delete" command does not actually remove data from a PC; the data continue to reside on the PC unless or until they are overwritten. Norton Utility is just one type of software that makes these data readily accessible.

- Pay attention to altered fields on documents, including whited-out or scribbled-over attempts to change information or make it unreadable. Documents that are so treated are obviously useful in pattern analysis.

- The telephone book and its cousin the Haines Directory (the criss-cross) can be simple and efficacious investigative tools, particularly when reinforced with imaginative telephone inquiry. In the hands of an experienced internal auditor and supplemented by information from other basic external sources such as Dun & Bradstreet and state records of incorporation, these basic tools can provide the essential external information necessary to identify the true identity and relationship of otherwise hidden ultimate payees.

- The order in which you interview employees is important. Usually, reserve prime suspects for last, and keep them apart from each other, both before and particularly after the interview. Do not let them know precisely how much and what information you actually have prior to the interviews.

- Do not dismiss employees too soon. This is a common error that frequently occurs through righteous indignation on the part of well-intended management or, occasionally, as the result of a less innocent managerial desire for damage control. The relevant legal principle is that an employee has a certain duty to respond to inquiries that a non-employee does not.

- Recognize the difference between an interview and an interrogation. The two involve very different approaches. An interview is open-ended, and the interviewer is essentially neutral. The purpose is to obtain information. An interrogation is accusatory, designed to elicit a confession. Further details are beyond the scope of this book; we refer you to Joseph Buckley of John E. Reid & Associates Inc., Chicago, for interesting and useful seminars on this topic.

- Furthermore, for legal reasons, do not ever physically block the subjects' free access route out of the interview area. You do not want to provide interview subjects with an excuse to contend that they were forcibly detained against their will, which would render inadmissible any information obtained in the interview.

- Obtain original documents and photocopy them twice—retain one clear copy as well as a working copy.

- Maintain a chain-of-custody evidence log from the beginning of the investigation. This basically serves to demonstrate that the custodianship for all physical evidence (i.e., documents) has been accounted for and asserts that the documents have not been tampered with (i.e., what you see is what we got).

- Document the management system, delineating the perpetrator's position, authority level (actual as well as per policy), and sphere of influence.

- If fidelity bond recovery is relevant, determine the requirements early. In particular, determine the documentary requirements. Do recognize, however, that a certain loss of control over the investigation may result when and if you involve the insurer. For example, the bonding company typically makes the call about when and whether to notify law enforcement.

- Recognize the advantages of a proactive antifraud program under sentencing guidelines, and use this to obtain resources from senior management. (Note that this was written before Sarbanes-Oxley; one expects that resources would be less of a problem in the current environment—but you may still want to lobby for broader fraud prevention efforts than just those directed at financial reporting.)

- Fraud is uncomfortable for the organization, and everyone wants answers and decisions sooner rather than later. Do not be pressured into taking less time than you need to thoroughly complete your investigation. This might be considered the cardinal rule of management fraud investigation: Senior management will always want—and expect—answers before the fraud investigation has run its course. You will need to carefully manage this process.

- An unfortunately necessary cautionary note: Expect to be attacked when conducting an investigation into management fraud. Such attacks are usually directed at the credibility of the audit and the auditors. Be prepared for this, and conduct yourself and the investigation in an above-board manner so as not to provide ammunition to those who have a vested interest in discrediting the process.

- Make an effort to avoid what Courtenay Thompson refers to as "tissue damage"—that is, actual physical risk to the auditors. Be sensible, and do not put yourself or others in harm's way. As a practical matter in certain investigations, you will need to be alert for this possibility. Bring your security department into the investigation if there is any question of risk.

CHAPTER 9

CAAT Scans for Scams

Because others have covered this topic thoroughly, this book will deal only relatively briefly with technology applications in recognizing fraud. For a comprehensive discussion of numerous ACL and CAAT fraud-related applications, see David Corderre's *Fraud Detection: Using Data Analysis Techniques to Detect Fraud.*[1] In addition, as this was being written, Professor Steve Albrecht was working on a new book that will address the topic of technology-based detection—what Albrecht calls "deductive investigation."

The process of deductive investigation as outlined by Albrecht and summarized here is similar, at least in principle, to our ideal approach:

Step 1. Understand the business.

Step 2. Identify possible fraud.

Step 3. Catalog possible fraud symptoms.

Step 4. Use technology to gather data about symptoms.

Step 5. Analyze results.

Step 6. Investigate symptoms and follow up/automate detection procedures.

In particular, we emphasize the need to both understand the business and catalog specific but meaningful symptoms. Using automated processes, the data should be analyzed to identify and then investigate the symptoms. The key is to set the symptom threshold such that false positives are kept to a manageable level, although they will not be completely eliminated.

Certain continuous monitoring routines that we employ are directed toward identification of patterns associated with the red flags of management fraud, while top-level forensic data analyses are directed at symptoms of potential financial-reporting manipulation. We also perform continuous monitoring that is designed to detect the telltale debits of misappropriation and the basic bank account matches (with one additional wrinkle). Because the routines explained here are less sophisticated and data-intensive than those recommended by Professor Albrecht, we refer readers to his text for a more thorough analysis.

MIDDLEMEN/RELATED PARTIES

One area on which to focus is patterns that point to potential middlemen or related parties inserted between a company and its real suppliers or customers. In general, when this occurs, the red flags to look for are margins, sales prices, or purchase costs that do not correspond to market value, typically coupled with inexplicably large volumes.

Use the following data analysis routines to identify these possibilities:

- Sales or purchases with unit values more than X standard deviations from all other transactions for that particular material or product (the amount represented by X will be a function of the specific business context).

- Margin analyses for sales to detect preferential treatment of potential middlemen by identifying anomalous low-margin sales. The other side of this coin is purchase price analyses to identify sore-thumb purchases at out-of-line costs.

- Bill-to versus ship-to address anomalies. One specific test identifies ship-to addresses from earlier periods with new bill-to addresses. However, note that a certain incidence level of these normally occurring patterns is expected. As with any form of pattern analysis, look for the unusual, sore-thumb level of occurrence.

- Volume stratification, in purchases and/or sales, in descending order for at least the last three years. Potential middlemen will appear seemingly out of nowhere.

- Unusual payment terms—either the extension of excessively lengthy credit terms or unusually early payment (without a justifying discount).

To follow up, obtain D&Bs, refer to state records of incorporation, use the telephone book (sometimes creatively) or Internet sources of information, or visit the address. Working with the security department can help to identify possible perpetrators.

Ongoing continuous monitoring of payments to consultants is also useful to detect potentially sensitive payments (i.e., fraud for the organization), as well as monitoring opportunities for personal enrichment by disguised payments to related parties. One useful tactic is to combine this with wire transfer monitoring, building in the additional criterion of an unusually high approval level for the transaction.

TOP-DOWN FORENSIC MONITORING

The section called "Financial Reporting" in Chapter 7 discussed forensic audit procedures directed at the top level of the financial-reporting process, suggesting that such procedures should include analyses of period-end, top-level journal entries, particularly those made to discretionary reserves. Following are examples of what could be done via continuous monitoring in this area.

Discretionary Reserves

- Identify those accounts that are similar in nature to discretionary reserves—or that could be a parking ground for material debits resulting from major period-end journal entries (à la WorldCom). Typically, these would include various discretionary reserves and certain major noncurrent asset accounts.

- Capture all general journal entries to these accounts with a P&L effect greater than $X (with X representing a very high threshold). The focus should be by account, groups of accounts, and entry(ies). The amount of X would be the P&L effect in the aggregate.

- Analyze the patterns vertically—that is, the effect on P&L for *that* month or quarter, and/or horizontally—the effect *across a time period* comprising multiple months or quarters.

- In theory, the extended time period is expected to provide the meaningful context within which patterns of financial-reporting manipulation are discernible—such as consistent adjustments to, say, reserves for environmental liabilities that might have the effect of adjusting earnings to "make the number."

Revenue Recognition

- For revenue overstatement via leaving the books open at the end of the accounting period, typical continuous monitoring flags include average daily sales more than X standard deviations higher than normal, followed by a corresponding drop in the average daily sales for the first part of the subsequent period, or average daily sales egregiously above the norm (well more than X standard deviations), coupled with accounting entries from atypical sources other than the invoicing system, for example, general journal entries.

- For channel stuffing, typical continuous monitoring flags include markedly increased returns after the period-end; considerably extended, out-of-the-ordinary (for those particular customers) credit terms; markedly increased discounts as compared to the norm for those customers; and other marked divergences from the norm for these types of transactions and customers.

- For swaps or reciprocal sales, continuous monitoring routines could involve identifying simultaneous major sales and purchases to and from the same company(ies) that were recorded via journal entries or out-of-the-ordinary billing/purchasing practices, particularly when such transactions were entered into at the same time, in similar amounts, and had other equal and offsetting aspects (e.g., the same unusual credit terms).

Continuous monitoring is designed to capture potential entries for careful, independent scrutiny. We suggest quarterly monitoring, rather than monthly, to provide a big-picture vantage point.

TELLTALE DEBITS OF MISAPPROPRIATION

The effects of asset misappropriation are normally recognizable on the books, hence the term *telltale debits*. Related to this is the concept of the *debit dumping ground*, wherein debits are accumulated in accounts that are not subjected to the customary accounting controls of analysis and comparison to the underlying assets. Debit dumping grounds can also crop up when there are buildups of excess credits that serve to offset and obscure the otherwise telltale debits.

These debits constitute the visible symptoms; the key is to design meaningful identification criteria. Such criteria usually involve patterns over time. One useful identifier is the source or originator of entries.

Following are examples of this type of continuous monitoring:

- *Clearance accounts.*   Many variations are possible here. The key is to identify patterns of debits that move out over time to an unreasonably aged status. This could indicate a debit dumping ground. Even more telling would be patterns of movement through various clearance accounts to avoid sore-thumb aging.

- *Escheatable funds.*   The pattern to look for here is eventual disposition by check other than to the indicated payee or the state—in particular, last-minute disbursements to payees other than the original payee, especially if these eleventh-hour payments are to the same payee.

- *Sundry other credits.*   This pattern is similar to the immediately preceding example: disbursements to payees other than the anticipated payee to clear balances.

- *Sundry other assets.*   Frequently, recorded accountability is weak for these generic accounts. As a result, they can serve as a catch-all for commingled, various-and-sundry debits. When this occurs, perpetrators of fraud, primarily of the accounting-cycle type, can take advantage. For these types of analyses, specific identifiers such as originator can identify unusual patterns that would otherwise exist below the radar. One very simple identifier is a list by amount and originator.

- *Miscellaneous expense.*   The same principles would apply here as for sundry assets. It is necessary to specify criteria in order to extract the pertinent information.

- *Credit memo debit offsets.*   Unusual patterns are all-important here: Look to originator, amounts, customer accounts, and the like.

These are just examples—the reader will get the picture readily. The key is to specify the right criteria in order to achieve meaningful screening and filtering but still keep false positives at a manageable level. Trial-and-error and adjustment of the thresholds may be useful over time—what Professor Albrecht refers to as the "follow up/automate detection procedures" step, which closes the continuous monitoring loop.

BANK ACCOUNTS/ADDRESSES

The standard computer-assisted-audit technique (CAAT) routines used to match employee addresses to vendor addresses (to detect bogus vendors), employee bank account numbers to vendor bank account numbers (again, to detect bogus vendors), and employee bank accounts to other employee bank accounts (to detect payroll fraud) are well documented. Refer to Corderre's *Fraud Detection*[2] for these and other useful CAATs.

There are two routines that have proved useful in matching addresses. The first was developed by Professor Mark Negrini. It employs computerized matching to identify "fuzzy addresses," a process whereby the software removes all of the nonnumeric characters and matches on the basis of, for example, street address and zip code. This routine matches "1021 West Able Street, Columbus, Ohio, 43205" and "1021 W. Able St., Columbus, OH 43205"; however, this routine also matches these to "1021 Front Street, Dublin, OH 43205."

The second routine supplements the standard comparison of employee to vendor addresses by comparing addresses for such items as certain employees' beneficiaries and employment application references—what are called the "once-removed" individuals. This information is available from human resource files. This extended comparison routine works for all accounts payable and payroll employees, and, more important, for business unit operating managers.

If you consider this routine to be a stretch, keep in mind that just such a match was the key to breaking a major management fraud some years ago, although it was performed manually at the time. In that case, the maiden name of the wife of the business unit president was the key to identifying a related party.

In addition, Professor Negrini has popularized audit applications of Benford's Law—expected frequencies of naturally occurring numbers to highlight apparent intervention or artificially created numbers.[3] My former company used Benford's Law more as a general risk indicator (a shotgun) than as a specific indicator (a rifle). In general, stratification of files based on amounts and analyses of patterns are probably more directly useful.

CHAPTER 10

Conclusion

LOW FREQUENCY OF DETECTION/PROSECUTION VERSUS EFFECTIVE PREVENTION

Effective prevention is dependent on the probability of detection and prosecution more than on any other single factor. Major management fraud, however, is significantly underdetected. Moreover, when this type of fraud is recognized, it is all too frequently not prosecuted. The risk/reward implications of underdetection and underprosecution are obvious.

Unsupported by much more than deductive reasoning, a considerable amount of experience, and a dash of intuition, we submit that a substantial amount of management fraud against the organization goes undetected. The major reason for this is because it is different from the on-the books, accounting-cycle-based fraud that most internal auditors are geared to recognize.

Related to that, and certainly less conjectural, is the simple observation that too much management fraud goes unprosecuted. Since *the most effective deterrent is the probability of detection and prosecution,* this has definite consequences. Certainly, operating-management fraud is underrepresented in the internal audit professional literature. About two years ago, while getting one of the information technology auditors started in our company's continuous monitoring program (which is directed at just this type of fraud), we ran into this lack of professional guidance. In fact, that void prompted this book.

The discussion of red flags in Chapter 4 hypothesized that financial-reporting and employee accounting-cycle types of fraud are well represented in the literature because they are *accounting-based* and fit into that established professional frame of reference. The more *managerial* aspects of operating fraud, however, do not fit neatly into a similar professional niche.

If you say "management fraud" to an average group of internal auditors, a considerable majority of them will think first of fraudulent financial reporting. The lack of recognition and attention accorded operating-management fraud against the organization might be a cause as well as a symptom of the prevailing climate of underdetection (although this is a chicken-and-egg situation). Refer to the section entitled "Managerial as Well as Accounting Perspective" later in this chapter for further comments on the primary reason for the underdetection of management non-financial-statement fraud.

You might ask: What about the ACFE "Reports to the Nation" and the 42 percent incidence of management fraud reported there? Surely that indicates a reasonable rate of detection? What it actually indicates is a realistic *ratio* between the reported instances of management fraud and those of employee fraud. The *number of instances reported, however, is quite small* for both categories. In fact, the number of reported instances of management fraud supports this hypothesis.

For the six-year period covered by the ACFE 2002 "Report to the Nation," approximately 10,000 certified fraud examiners (CFEs) were surveyed. Only 663 cases were reported for this period.[1] That's an average of 110.5 per year, of which only 46.4 were instances of management fraud. Considering the fact that the CFEs specialize in fraud, the recognition/detection/investigation glass appears to be not even half full. (Admittedly, using the ACFE report data in this fashion is simplistic and somewhat out of context.) Please see the section "History: Good Old Days" for another reason to assume that the rate of detection would have gone down from a low base to start with.

Two basic factors get in the way of consistent, effective prosecution:

1. Just as it is more difficult to recognize management non-financial-statement fraud, it is likewise more difficult to prove. Because these frauds frequently happen off the books, it can be more difficult to obtain support when conducting an investigation. There is also the difficulty of presenting the frequently complex issues so that a jury can understand the case. Moreover, there is the *ambiguity of management fraud:* Is it the result of stupidity or cupidity? Is it just an unintended consequence of mismanagement, waste, or abuse, or did the manager in question engage in the criminal activity with the intent to deceive and for personal gain?

2. Yielding to blackmail by electing not to prosecute someone who has damaging information about the company has the effect of encouraging fraud in the future. However, if your company does not have a firm policy stating that you will prosecute in all cases, you will have difficulty with the typical corporate legal department in getting effective action when someone attempts to use this tactic.

A related factor is simply corporate embarrassment. Personal issues may also interfere with the drive to prosecute, particularly if the fraud suspect worked in upper management. These personal factors may include denial resulting from a reluctance to believe in the perpetrator's guilt, which leaves gullible colleagues groping for mitigating factors; however, a failure to prosecute may also be the result of simple cronyism.

MANAGERIAL AS WELL AS ACCOUNTING PERSPECTIVE

This book has already described the differences between managerial operating fraud and employee accounting-cycle fraud. To summarize, operating-management fraud involves a conflict of interest and is off the books and relational; employee (or asset-misappropriation) fraud is on the books and transactional. From a traditional internal audit standpoint, instances of employee fraud are obviously more easily recognized and more likely to be encountered during the typical audit.

Recognition of management fraud requires a broader perspective than just determining that the transactions are recorded correctly and that the system of internal accounting control ensures such protocols as the segregation of duties and stratified authorizations. We saw earlier that performance accountability from a market-based normative perspective is required—for example, not just determining whether the P&L is recorded correctly, but also considering what the P&L should be. It is worth noting that this is also the most effective approach for recognizing fraudulent financials.

Recognition of management fraud is a process that focuses on the dynamics of profitability for the specific business. Auditors—even those who are typically much more experienced than the pass-through, two-years-and-out staff at many companies and who specialize in particular lines of business—should focus on recorded results in the context of the particular market. In terms of operating-management fraud, these auditors are looking for diverted or imported profits or understated or excessive charges from a normative viewpoint. The question they must ask is: What should the recorded results really be?

It is a good idea to supplement each internal audit project team by having the businesses involved nominate a go-to person who is responsible for providing the more nuanced business context and market information. Moreover, potential middleman companies should be monitored by data analyses of volumes and specific margins. As discussed in Chapter 9, a senior data analyst can provide expertise in this area for every project. From there, it is a matter of recognizing red flags and major symptoms and *requiring* resolution of all indicated anomalies (budget be damned).

For diverted profits, the situation is analogous to Conan Doyle's aforementioned "dog that didn't bark." Very simply, the auditor should be aware of "missing profits." In addition, auditors must be aware of windfall profits that are on the books, inasmuch as these can offset excess charges, leaving a seemingly adequate net profitability. Obviously, an essential ingredient in this process is an in-depth understanding of the dynamics of a particular market in terms of prices, costs, and margins.

Four case studies from Chapter 5 are illustrative:

- See "Gouging the Customers" for an example of diverting windfall profits while leaving an adequate recorded profit.

- See "The Beach Club" for an example of how excess costs can be added to one business unit and then passed to others through transfer costs.

- See "He Was Just Like You and Me" for an example of how excess credits on the books can obscure excess charges.

- See "Gouging the Customers" for an example of how cutouts can obscure market prices.

Consider also a case that was recently encountered on an audit and that demonstrates the market-based analysis we expect. This is a real-life situation and, as this is being written, the outcome is uncertain.

An audit team is auditing an operation in Asia. The business unit is buying from local trading companies rather than directly from the manufacturers. The explanation is that the local traders are maintaining inventories for the company, similar to just-in-time arrangements. The auditors have noted that the cost is less than the global benchmark costs that the international purchasing group distributes worldwide as a reference. On the face of it, everything looks okay.

However, the audit manager recognized these additional factors:

- Asia is now the low-cost producer for these materials.

- The global benchmark costs are based on U.S. costs, and an allowance for freight and customs is added. They have not been updated to reflect the emergence of the lower-cost Asian producers.

- For this location, the costs are just under the benchmark costs. The manager believes that *they should be 20 percent lower.*

The follow-up process is ongoing, and the outcome is uncertain. Experience suggests that 90 percent of the initially indicated anomalies will turn out to have a valid explanation. The audit team's responsibility, however, is first to recognize the anomalies and, second, to follow through to prove or disprove the indicated possibilities.

The process depends on *recognition (from a broad managerial perspective) of the possibilities,* and then *allocation of sufficient resources to effectively resolve the issue,* to either disprove the fraudulent possibilities or recommend an investigation. As noted in Chapter 1, the Institute of Internal Auditors says, "Detection of fraud consists of identifying indicators of fraud sufficient to warrant recommending an investigation."[2]

HISTORY: GOOD OLD DAYS

At risk of being labeled a dinosaur, let me take you down memory lane. Like those old-timers who walked to school barefoot in a blizzard, five miles and uphill both ways, I believe things were better then when it comes to the possibility of detecting operating-management fraud. Truth be told, most internal audit departments probably never really geared up to effectively detect management non-financial-statement fraud. However, if asked, most would have answered that they were looking real hard . . . and they had just the grizzled veterans who knew how to do it.

After the FCPA in 1977, many medium-sized companies had to quickly acquire an audit department. Public accounting became the source for many overnight internal auditors—so much so that, by the mid-1980s, the profession was inundated with former public accountants. On balance, this was not a bad thing. However, it had a definite effect on fraud auditing.

Quite simply, although they share some common ground, the two professions, internal audit and public accounting, are, in fact, distinctly different. However, perhaps because many former public accountants previously looked down on internal auditors (trust me on this—I spent six years in public accounting and management consulting), they proceeded to make over some aspects of the profession in their own (former) image.

The relevance of this is that public accounting, for reasons largely having to do with avoidance of legal liability, had always denied responsibility for detecting fraud. Couple this with their worship of budget efficiency, and pretty soon internal auditors were no longer gearing up to detect operating-management fraud, nor were they making any pretense about it.

When the 1990s arrived, things got worse. At most companies, internal audit departments were downsized, and, later, many were outsourced. Furthermore, the limited detection efforts that had existed back in the good old days were not particularly effective at most companies to begin with. Thus, what would have been the perceived risk of detection on the part of operating managers about to commit fraud in, say, 2000? They would have liked their chances, particularly considering the payoff.

THE RISK/REWARD DYNAMIC

Reward

As noted throughout this book, the most effective deterrent of fraud is the probability of detection and prosecution. For the perpetrator, that's the *risk* part of the risk/reward equation.

The probability of detection has always been much lower for operating-management fraud than for employee accounting-cycle fraud, for reasons already discussed. Thus, we would have expected that part of the equation always to tilt toward taking the limited risk. So what has changed to alter the equation? By and large, the rewards have gone up considerably, the risk of detection diminished somewhat, and the perceived risk of prosecution (at least until recently) would have been markedly reduced, thanks to the leverage potential of employees "having something on the company."

In his "infectious greed" speech, Alan Greenspan said the latter half of the

1990s provided "an outsized increase in opportunities for avarice." Greenspan was talking about CEOs and senior management, particularly stock-option-driven managed earnings and abuse at the top. In addition to managed earnings and aggressive accounting, the magnitude of the conflict of interest, waste, and abuse visible at the top managerial levels certainly increased the perceived reward (the payoff) for the would-be fraud perpetrator at the operating-management level. Very simply, the rewards from operating fraud were greater than they ever had been

As noted previously, the perception has always been that the risk of detection and prosecution is fairly low. How did this change in the late 1990s? In terms of detection, not much (although there was some change—see "History: Good Old Days" earlier in this chapter); in terms of prosecution, things have changed a fair amount.

This book has chanted the mantra that fraud for the organization leads to fraud against the organization. Specifically, the dynamic whereby an employee has some detrimental information about the company or a superior, coupled with the opportunity to keep the effect of the fraud off the P&L, effectively leads to flaunting. By the end of the 1990s, many companies were engaged in much more questionable practices that lent themselves to such employee blackmail. Moreover, when people perceive that everyone around them is getting rich, the "infectious" part of infectious greed is more likely to take over.

Consider one other dimension of operating-management fraud: Not only is it larger and more complex, but it lasts longer. To paraphrase Warren Buffett in reference to misleading financial reporting, we are in the spin-cycle part of coming clean, and some laundry is dirtier than other laundry. It is quite possible that a *lot* of major operating-management fraud still remains to go through the spin cycle. The ominous implication for all of us in the profession is, how many instances will never be recognized?

The Fraud Triangle as Model

You are probably familiar with the classic model of fraud, the Fraud Triangle, developed by pioneering criminologist Donald Cressey.[3] This model is based on Cressey's interviews in the early 1950s with imprisoned bank embezzlers, whom Cressey referred to as "trust violators." His subjects were all first-time offenders, and what fascinated Cressey was the issue of how these formerly law-abiding citizens ended up committing the major crime of embezzlement. (For his research, he first eliminated those relatively few offenders who had taken their jobs with the express purpose of stealing.)

Cressey came away from his interviews with the important concept of the "nonsharable financial problem," which he thought drove his subjects to commit their crimes. From this, he constructed the classic Fraud Triangle shown in Exhibit 10.1. In this diagram, *opportunity* relates to internal control weaknesses, *need* is the nonsharable financial problem, and *rationalization* is the process whereby the aspiring perpetrator overcomes his (in those days the perpetrator was always male) personal ethical objections to the fraudulent act.

This dynamic fit the employee asset misappropriations of that time. In the intervening 50-plus years, other researchers have tweaked the model; however, Cressey's Fraud Triangle is still considered to be the operative occupational fraud model. Witness a recent (early 2003) joint venture between the American Institute of Certified Public Accountants (AICPA) and the ACFE to increase the awareness of fraud, which uses the Fraud Triangle as the model.

Although this model may still be appropriate for employee asset misappropriations, it really does not fit most major (million-dollar-plus) management fraud, particularly the corruption schemes. For starters, major management fraud usually involves overrides, rather than taking advantage

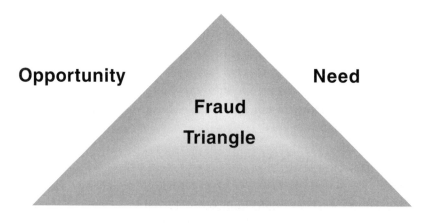

EXHIBIT 10.1   The Fraud Triangle

of an internal control weakness. Moreover, the aspect of a nonsharable financial problem is not usually present. Finally, although the world might be a simpler and more pleasant place if rationalization were still a requisite, in the early twenty-first century, it's just not the same hurdle for many, if not most, individuals, given the size of the potential rewards.

So what is the relevant current model for major management fraud? Earlier, this book discussed the risk/reward dynamic, with two risk dimensions: that of detection and that of prosecution. Furthermore, two important recurring factors were present in the various case study examples:

1. Major management fraud against the organization was frequently off the P&L, thereby avoiding detection.

2. An important dynamic in fraud against the organization was the belief by the perpetrator that, even if the fraud were to be detected, it would not be prosecuted.

Thus, the risk of detection and the risk of prosecution constitute the risk dynamic in major management fraud.

Deterrence

This chapter has already examined the management fraud risk/reward model in a historical context as it relates to the increased rewards and the decreased risks of detection and prosecution, and it considered the implications. What can be done now to tilt the balance back in favor of deterrence?

If we are going to reduce the incidence of major management fraud, particularly corruption by operating managers, we must increase the risk of detection *and* the risk of prosecution. In addition to enhanced internal audit capability, what else will change this dynamic? The Sarbanes-Oxley emphasis on code-of-ethics provisions will have a significant impact, particularly if one particular step is added: requiring an affirmation that the respondents are not aware of any illegal or unethical behavior, and if they are, details must be provided. Based on the author's personal observations and discussions with others in the profession, there is emerging evidence that such a requirement can be particularly efficacious in bringing complex cases of fraud to the forefront.

Sarbanes-Oxley required the SEC to issue disclosure rules for companies to report that they have instituted a code of ethics for the principle financial officers—and if not, why not—thereby ensuring that such codes will be adopted. In its proposed rule addressing this issue on October 16, 2002, the SEC indicated it would adopt the Sarbanes-Oxley requirements and, further, would require companies to report all waivers from the code granted to any of the officers.

The New York Stock Exchange (NYSE) has taken this a step further by simply requiring all of its listed companies to require a code of business conduct and ethics and to disclose all waivers granted to executive officers or directors. The NYSE will require various topics to be included, the most significant of which is to *encourage the reporting of illegal or unethical behavior* [emphasis ours]. As indicated, this last step is extremely important; over time, this practice could have a powerful effect on the perceived risk of detection on the part of managerial perpetrators of fraud.

Further, if we all broaden our perspectives to include nonaccounting symptoms and red flags, and consider the concepts that explain how major management fraud occurs, we can enhance the recognition process and, coupled with code-of-ethics reporting of wrongdoing, significantly increase the perpetrator's risk of detection.

As to the risk of prosecution, the heightened awareness accompanying Sarbanes-Oxley will have a much more salutary effect on corporate prosecutorial zeal in the future. All of us in the profession have seen a virtual groundswell, an emerging seriousness of purpose, frequently audit-committee-driven, of ethical behavior extending beyond mere compliance.

The wind is now at our backs. Good luck in your efforts at enhanced recognition. If you look hard into some of the areas that you may not be looking into now, you may be surprised at what you recognize. Simply put, detection and prosecution equal deterrence.

THOUGHTS ON RECENT ACCOUNTING SCANDALS

This section examines four of the most prominent corporate accounting scandals—which actually involve more corporate accountability than corporate accounting issues. These four instances involved different blends of aggressive/fraudulent financial reporting and managerial corruption, primarily based in conflicts of interest. The common element among all of them is a breach of trust on the part of senior management, coupled with an abdication of corporate governance by the boards of directors.

In one instance, whether or not the particular accounting transactions crossed the line into financial fraud was initially disputed by the company (Tyco). At this point, however, this has been all but admitted. What was never seriously in doubt was that the imperial CEO had systematically looted the company to the tune of $600 million.

Another case involved misleading financial reporting at least as much as fraudulent financial reporting (Enron). However, the popular myth that Enron was not technically in violation of GAAP is false—they were, in at least three areas.

One more scandal primarily entailed looting of the company and was only secondarily a case of financial-reporting fraud (Adelphia). And then there was the egregious violation of basic bookkeeping committed by WorldCom—the largest case of fraudulent financial reporting in U.S. business history.

As the Business Roundtable stated in reference to Enron, all of these high-profile instances of management fraud and abuse appeared ". . . to derive fundamentally from a massive *breach of trust.*" This, of course, is what management fraud is all about.

Tyco

If you believed the Tyco-sponsored special investigation, while the company engaged in aggressive financial reporting, this did not constitute "systemic or significant fraud." Finally, however, in July 2003, the company announced it was restating 5½ years of financial results.

The investigation was commissioned by the company and conducted by an independent law firm assisted by a forensic accounting firm. The special investigation report did describe various aggressive accounting practices employed to maximize reported profits and acknowledged that reported results for fiscal year 2002 were overstated by $382.2 million due to accounting errors.

In April 2003, the company reported pretax charges of $1.6 billion for accounting errors, almost all of which related to prior years. At that time, however, the company said that a restatement was not necessary (most accounting experts differed). The SEC apparently also had a different opinion, because Tyco finally restated prior years' earnings in July 2003. The restatements reduced pretax profits by $1.15 billion for fiscal years 1998 through 2001, and increased fiscal year 2002 pretax earnings by $183 million.

Regardless of whether you believe that Tyco's aggressive accounting rose to the level of fraud, there is no doubt that the former CEO, Dennis Kozlowski, engaged in massive conflict of interest. Kozlowski and two other officers were charged with stealing $170 million via company loans and fraudulent sales of securities amounting to $430 million.

This investigation began in January 2002, based on a tip alleging fraudulent financial reporting by the company. The investigative trail first led to personal purchases of art by Kozlowski, allegedly using company funds. In June 2002, Kozlowski was indicted for evading sales taxes on the art purchases, and he resigned at that time.

In September 2002, the SEC filed civil fraud charges against Kozlowski and two other executives. "Kozlowski [and the other two officers] treated Tyco as their private bank, taking out hundreds of millions of dollars of loans and compensation without ever telling investors," said Stephen Cutler, SEC director of enforcement.

The SEC complaint was filed simultaneously with criminal charges brought by the Manhattan district attorney. Allegations included hundreds of dollars in low- or no-interest loans granted without board-of-directors approval, many of which were subsequently forgiven, again with neither board approval nor disclosure to investors. These "forgiven" loans were also not reported for tax purposes, leading to recent indictments for tax evasion.

Kozlowski and the two officers were also charged with misappropriating $20 million by directing a payment to a board director without notifying or obtaining approval from the other members of the board.

Enron

As stated in the preface to this book, "Enron had all of the elements and dynamics commented upon herein . . . because it was first an overarching management fraud and only secondly a financial reporting fraud."

Enron touched all the bases: fraud *for* the organization (financial reporting fraud, illegal dealings to take advantage of the California energy crisis, accusations of bribery of three NatWest employees, etc.), corruption and conflict-of-interest fraud *against* the organization (numerous examples of alleged self-dealing by a number of top Enron executives), and, of course, the infamous document shredding involving Arthur Andersen, Enron's auditors.

The financial-reporting fraud was perhaps noteworthy for the extent to which it was aided by the external auditors, other financial advisors, and, most significantly, Enron's bankers. The primary method was the considerable use of complex so-called special-purpose entities (SPEs) to keep debt off Enron's books. By misuse of this tactic, Enron was able to keep the full extent of its debt hidden and manipulate off-the-books transactions in order to create on-the-books income.

In July 2003, Citigroup and J.P. Morgan settled with the SEC by agreeing to pay $305 million in respect of loans and trades that had the effect of "helping to commit a fraud." Specifically, the settlement related to $8.3 billion in loans improperly accounted for. The effect of these off-the-books loans was to boost Enron's cash flow, while hiding the actual nature of the transaction.

Enron also used the SPEs to handsomely reward its chosen top executives via blatant conflict-of-interest arrangements permitting self-dealing. (In fact, the board granted two exemptions to the company code-of-ethics policy to permit CFO Andrew Fastow to engage in SPE conflicts of interest). Further, Enron was able to syndicate profitable off-the-books partnerships to reward (and co-opt) useful alliances in the financial community.

Adelphia

Whereas the Enron scandal primarily involved fraudulent financial reporting and only secondarily fraud against the organization, Adelphia reversed that pattern. The primary factor was massive fraud against the organization (blatant conflict of interest) that resulted in fraudulent reporting.

Over a multiyear period, the Rigas family and their family-owned partnerships received $3.1 billion in company-guaranteed loans that were not recorded in the books of the company. In addition, numerous personal use of company funds (e.g., to build a personal golf course) were eventually reported. Unfortunately, for the family and for the company, a substantial amount of the loan proceeds was used to buy Adelphia stock, which subsequently suffered a marked decline in market value.

The company ended up having to restate its books for the preceding three years to recognize the liabilities. The patriarch of the family became the first high-profile CEO to do the "perpwalk" for national TV.

WorldCom

Simultaneously the largest bankruptcy and largest financial-reporting fraud in U.S. history, the WorldCom fraud was also perhaps the simplest of major U.S. accounting frauds. As of August 2003, the estimate of the accounting "errors" was nearly $12 billion. At this point, the Justice Department has filed criminal charges against several company managers, some of whom have pleaded guilty.

The accounting fraud primarily related to capitalization of so-called line charges (payments to other phone companies for connections to complete calls). Instead of charging these costs to current operations, WorldCom elected to capitalize these as long-term investments, contrary to GAAP. Given the pattern and timing of the amounts fraudulently capitalized, the intent was clear: to camouflage the continuing significant shortfall in earnings (which were contrary to the heady expectations).

As just about everyone in the United States now knows, the initially identified $3.8 billion overcapitalization was discovered by the WorldCom internal auditors as part of an ostensibly routine internal audit. (The author suspects that the auditors had been tipped and are still protecting the identity of the tipster.)

The vice president of internal audit, Cynthia Cooper, became one of the three *Time* magazine "Persons of the Year"—and deservedly so. She demonstrated professional and personal courage by persevering in the face of considerable pressure by the CFO, first to drop and then later to delay the audit. Interestingly enough, if the CFO had been permitted to delay the audit, he conceivably would have been successful in sweeping the fraudulently capitalized charges under the rug as part of a much larger write-off of goodwill that was to occur as of June 30.

In this case, the fraudulent financial reporting dwarfs other fraud manifestations; however, there were other, lesser offenses reported in the financial press, such as systematic overbillings of customer phone charges and, recently, alleged misbillings to other carriers. Allegedly, WorldCom systematically hid the nature of long-distance calls that were rerouted through other carriers so that they appeared to be local calls, in order to avoid having to pay access charges.

Finally, the CEO was the beneficiary of $1 billion in personal and business loans from the company. As distinct from the Tyco case, however, these loans were approved by the (perhaps overly compliant) board . . . and not forgiven.

Practice Advisory 1210.A2-1: Identification of Fraud

Interpretation of Standard 1210.A2 from the *Standards for the Professional Practice of Internal Auditing*

RELATED STANDARD: 1210.A2

The internal auditor should have sufficient knowledge to identify the indicators of fraud but is not expected to have the expertise of a person whose primary responsibility is detecting and investigating fraud.

Nature of This Practice Advisory

Internal auditors should consider the following suggestions in connection with the identification of fraud. This guidance is not intended to represent all the considerations that may be necessary, but simply a recommended set of items that should be addressed. Compliance with Practice Advisories is optional.

1. Fraud encompasses an array of irregularities and illegal acts characterized by intentional deception. It can be perpetrated for the benefit of or to the detriment of the organization and by persons outside as well as inside the organization.

2. Fraud designed to benefit the organization generally produces such benefit by exploiting an unfair or dishonest advantage that also may

deceive an outside party. Perpetrators of such fraud usually accrue an indirect personal benefit. Examples of fraud designed to benefit the organization include:

- Sale or assignment of fictitious or misrepresented assets.
- Improper payments such as illegal political contributions, bribes, kickbacks, and payoffs to government officials, intermediaries of government officials, customers, or suppliers.
- Intentional, improper representation or valuation of transactions, assets, liabilities, or income.
- Intentional, improper transfer pricing (e.g., valuation of goods exchanged between related organizations). By purposely structuring pricing techniques improperly, management can improve the operating results of an organization involved in the transaction to the detriment of the other organization.
- Intentional, improper related-party transactions in which one party receives some benefit not obtainable in an arm's-length transaction.
- Intentional failure to record or disclose significant information to improve the financial picture of the organization to outside parties.
- Prohibited business activities such as those that violate government statutes, rules, regulations, or contracts.
- Tax fraud.

3. Fraud perpetrated to the detriment of the organization generally is for the direct or indirect benefit of an employee, an outside individual, or another organization. Some examples are:

- Acceptance of bribes or kickbacks
- Diversion to an employee or outsider of a potentially profitable transaction that would normally generate profits for the organization
- Embezzlement, as typified by the misappropriation of money or property, and falsification of financial records to cover up the act, thus making detection difficult
- Intentional concealment or misrepresentation of events or data
- Claims submitted for services or goods not actually provided to the organization

4. Deterrence of fraud consists of those actions taken to discourage the perpetration of fraud and limit the exposure if fraud does occur. The principal mechanism for deterring fraud is control. Primary responsibility for establishing and maintaining control rests with management.

5. Internal auditors are responsible for assisting in the deterrence of fraud by examining and evaluating the adequacy and the effectiveness of the system of internal control, commensurate with the extent of the potential exposure/risk in the various segments of the organization's operations. In carrying out this responsibility, internal auditors should, for example, determine whether:

   - The organizational environment fosters control consciousness.
   - Realistic organizational goals and objectives are set.
   - Written policies (e.g., code of conduct) exist that describe prohibited activities and the action required whenever violations are discovered.
   - Appropriate authorization policies for transactions are established and maintained.
   - Policies, practices, procedures, reports, and other mechanisms are developed to monitor activities and safeguard assets, particularly in high-risk areas.
   - Communication channels provide management with adequate and reliable information.
   - Recommendations need to be made for the establishment or enhancement of cost-effective controls to help deter fraud.

6. When an internal auditor suspects wrongdoing, the appropriate authorities within the organization should be informed. The internal auditor may recommend whatever investigation is considered necessary in the circumstances. Thereafter, the auditor should follow up to see that the internal auditing activity's responsibilities have been met.

7. Investigation of fraud consists of performing extended procedures necessary to determine whether fraud, as suggested by the indicators, has occurred. It includes gathering sufficient information about the specific details of a discovered fraud. Internal auditors, lawyers, investigators, security personnel, and other specialists from inside or outside the organization are the parties that usually conduct or participate in fraud investigations.

8. When conducting fraud investigations, internal auditors should:

   - Assess the probable level and the extent of complicity in the fraud within the organization. This can be critical to ensuring that the internal auditor avoids providing information to or obtaining misleading information from persons who may be involved.
   - Determine the knowledge, skills, and other competencies needed to carry out the investigation effectively. An assessment of the qualifications and the skills of internal auditors and of the specialists available to participate in the investigation should be performed to ensure that engagements are conducted by individuals having appropriate types and levels of technical expertise. This should include assurances on such matters as professional certifications, licenses, reputation, and the fact that there is no relationship to those being investigated or to any of the employees or management of the organization.
   - Design procedures to follow in attempting to identify the perpetrators, extent of the fraud, techniques used, and cause of the fraud.
   - Coordinate activities with management personnel, legal counsel, and other specialists as appropriate throughout the course of the investigation.
   - Be cognizant of the rights of alleged perpetrators and personnel within the scope of the investigation and the reputation of the organization itself.

9. Once a fraud investigation is concluded, internal auditors should assess the facts known in order to:

   - Determine if controls need to be implemented or strengthened to reduce future vulnerability.
   - Design engagement tests to help disclose the existence of similar fraud in the future.
   - Help meet the internal auditor's responsibility to maintain sufficient knowledge of fraud and thereby be able to identify future indicators of fraud.

10. Reporting of fraud consists of the various oral or written, interim or final communications to management regarding the status and results of fraud investigations. The chief audit executive has the responsibility to

report immediately any incident of significant fraud to senior management and the board. Sufficient investigation should take place to establish reasonable certainty that a fraud has occurred before any fraud reporting is made. A preliminary or final report may be desirable at the conclusion of the detection phase. The report should include the internal auditor's conclusion as to whether sufficient information exists to conduct a full investigation. It should also summarize observations and recommendations that serve as the basis for such decision. A written report may follow any oral briefing made to management and the board to document the findings.

11. Section 2400 of the *Standards* provides interpretations applicable to engagement communications issued as a result of fraud investigations. Additional interpretive guidance on reporting of fraud is as follows:

    • When the incidence of significant fraud has been established to a reasonable certainty, senior management and the board should be notified immediately.

    • The results of a fraud investigation may indicate that fraud has had a previously undiscovered significant adverse effect on the financial position and results of operations of an organization for one or more years on which financial statements have already been issued. Internal auditors should inform senior management and the board of such a discovery.

    • A written report or other formal communication should be issued at the conclusion of the investigation phase. It should include all observations, conclusions, recommendations, and corrective action taken.

    • A draft of the proposed final communications on fraud should be submitted to legal counsel for review. In those cases in which the internal auditor wants to invoke client privilege, consideration should be given to addressing the report to legal counsel.

12. Detection of fraud consists of identifying indicators of fraud sufficient to warrant recommending an investigation. These indicators may arise as a result of controls established by management, tests conducted by auditors, and other sources both within and outside the organization.

13. In conducting engagements, the internal auditor's responsibilities for detecting fraud are to:

- Have sufficient knowledge of fraud to be able to identify indicators that fraud may have been committed. This knowledge includes the need to know the characteristics of fraud, the techniques used to commit fraud, and the types of fraud associated with the activities reviewed.
- Be alert to opportunities, such as control weaknesses, that could allow fraud. If significant control weaknesses are detected, additional tests conducted by internal auditors should include tests directed toward identification of other indicators of fraud. Some examples of indicators are unauthorized transactions, override of controls, unexplained pricing exceptions, and unusually large product losses. Internal auditors should recognize that the presence of more than one indicator at any one time increases the probability that fraud may have occurred.
- Evaluate the indicators that fraud may have been committed and decide whether any further action is necessary or whether an investigation should be recommended.
- Notify the appropriate authorities within the organization if a determination is made that there are sufficient indicators of the commission of a fraud to recommend an investigation.

14. Internal auditors are not expected to have knowledge equivalent to that of a person whose primary responsibility is detecting and investigating fraud. Also, audit procedures alone, even when carried out with due professional care, do not guarantee that fraud will be detected.

Practice Advisory 1210.A2-2: Responsibility for Fraud Detection

Interpretation of Standard 1210.A2 from the *Standards for the Professional Practice of Internal Auditing*

RELATED STANDARD: 1210.A2

The internal auditor should have sufficient knowledge to identify the indicators of fraud but is not expected to have the expertise of a person whose primary responsibility is detecting and investigating fraud.

Nature of This Practice Advisory

Internal auditors should consider the following suggestions in relation to the responsibility for fraud detection. This guidance is not intended to represent all the considerations that may be necessary, but is simply a recommended set of items that should be addressed. Compliance with Practice Advisories is optional.

1. Management and the internal audit activity have differing roles with respect to fraud detection. The normal course of work for the internal audit activity is to provide an independent appraisal, examination, and evaluation of an organization's activities as a service to the organization. The objective of internal auditing in fraud detection is to assist members of the organization in the effective discharge of their respon-

sibilities by furnishing them with analyses, appraisals, recommendations, counsel, and information concerning the activities reviewed. The engagement objective includes promoting effective control at a reasonable cost.

2. Management has a responsibility to establish and maintain an effective control system at a reasonable cost. To the degree that fraud may be present in activities covered in the normal course of work as defined above, internal auditors have a responsibility to exercise "due professional care" as specifically defined in *Standard 1220* with respect to fraud detection. Internal auditors should have sufficient knowledge of fraud to identify the indicators that fraud may have been committed, be alert to opportunities that could allow fraud, evaluate the need for additional investigation, and notify the appropriate authorities.

3. A well-designed internal control system should not be conducive to fraud. Tests conducted by auditors, along with reasonable controls established by management, improve the likelihood that any existing fraud indicators will be detected and considered for further investigation.

Derivation: Management Non-Financial-Statement Fraud as a Percentage of Total Occupational Fraud Loss

The ACFE 1996 "Report to the Nation" was used for these derivations because much more data are currently available from that study than from the 2002 report. (The 2002 report data are consistent with the 1996 report data for this purpose.)

Assume 100 frauds in the relative frequency and cost of the ACFE 1996 "Report to the Nation":

1. Eliminate financial-statement fraud. Assume that 80 percent of these are performed by the executive group, and 20 percent by managers. (Based on the ACFE report, the incidence of financial-statement fraud is 5 percent. The 1999 COSO report on fraudulent financial reporting indicated that approximately 83 percent of these were attributable to the CEO and/or CFO.)

2. The incidence of executive non-financial-statement fraud then becomes 8 percent and managerial fraud becomes 29 percent (the 12 percent of the ACFE report less the 4 percent assumed to be financial-statement fraud, and the ACFE's 30 percent less 1 percent).

3. Assume (conservatively) the median loss for the remaining executive fraud instances is now $500,000. (The ACFE report had this median loss as $1 million; however, this included financial-reporting frauds.)

Then, using the respective median loss by employment-category amounts (the ACFE report does not provide the mean) as proxies for the mean, the following rough approximation can be derived:

	Incidence	Loss/ incident	Total loss	% of total
Executive	8	$500,000	$4,000,000	
Managerial	29	250,000	7,250,000	
Total Managerial Fraud	**37**		**$11,250,000**	76%
Employee Fraud	58	$60,000	3,480,000	24%
Total Fraud	**95**		**$14,730,000**	**100%**

Conclusion: The total loss from management fraud is approximately 75 percent of the loss from non-financial-statement occupational fraud (conservatively).

Percentage of Total Occupational Fraud Loss Attributable to Management Fraud

T he information in this appendix is an estimate based on estimates; it neither seeks nor implies precision. Rather, it offers rough relative percentages and orders of magnitude.

The ACFE 1996 "Report to the Nation" commingled the *amount of loss* to the organization from non-financial-statement fraud with the *amount of misstatement* resulting from financial-reporting fraud. Consequently, this writer believes the report overstates the effect of fraudulent reporting by a considerable extent.

Incidentally, this might be part of the reason that the ACFE estimates that organizations lose about 6 percent of their total revenue to all forms of fraud. To many of us, 6 percent of revenues appears excessive as an estimate of total loss from occupational fraud.

To begin with, consider the 1999 COSO report on fraudulent financial reporting occurring during an 11-year period from January 1987 through December 1997. This report found almost 300 instances of such fraud and studied approximately 200. The results:

- The median misstatement or asset misappropriation was only $4.1 million; the average, however, was $25 million.

- The relatively small losses were because most of these companies were comparatively small (78 percent were not listed on either the NYSE or the American Stock Exchange, and the typical size was less than $100 million in total assets).[1]

Recognizing that the median amount of fraud loss is going to be less than the average, the *total* amount for these 300 cases *over the 11-year period* would be *only approximately $7.5 billion,* which is a far cry from what the ACFE is projecting.

A more meaningful measurement for financial-statement fraud is the loss to investors. Former SEC chief accountant Lynn Turner has estimated that amount as $100 billion for the six-year period from 1996 through 2001. For perspective, the total P&L effect of the 463 restatements in 1998, 1999, and 2000 was $5.8 billion. By 2000, however, the loss to investors was over $30 billion.

If we use $30 billion as the annual loss to investors in a typical year from financial-reporting fraud and 1.5 percent for the estimated loss from all forms of occupational fraud, we can apply that to the GNP of the U.S. economy. Then, we can derive the amount as follows ($ billions):

Total loss from occupational fraud (1.5 percent of $10 trillion)	$150.0
Loss from fraudulent financials	30.0
Difference: non-financial-statement loss	$120.0
Conservative estimate of management non-financial-statement fraud (1)	$90.0
Estimate of employee non-financial-statement fraud	30.0
	$120.0 (2)

1. Based on conservative estimate of 3-to-1 (75 percent) derived in Appendix C.

2. *Occupational Fraud and Abuse* estimates the loss from bribery and corruption as 52 percent of the total loss from non-financial-statement fraud. So, in this example, the loss from bribery and corruption would be $62.4 billion; the loss from asset misappropriation would be $57.6 billion.

The portion of total loss attributable to management non-financial-statement fraud in this example is 60 percent. This represents a majority of all fraud loss.

If we accept the "normal" annual loss to investors of $30 billion, the only way that management non-financial-statement fraud would not be a majority of the total loss from all forms of occupational fraud would be *if the overall total loss were less than 1 percent of total revenue.*

Please note that, since management fraud and corruption are more difficult to detect (and are doubtless underreported), the true percentage of loss resulting from management bribery and corruption would be something in excess of the preceding estimates.

KPMG Study

KPMG surveyed 5,000 U.S. publicly held companies, government organizations, and not-for-profit entities in 1998 and issued a report on occupational fraud in 1999. (As of August 2003, this study had not been updated.)[1] We have broken down their reported fraud classifications into the three broad categories of the ACFE reports and separated external fraud.

We have added the category of fraud for the organization to capture the nature of false financial statements. (In so doing, we recognize the dual nature of bid rigging/price-fixing, which can be fraud *for* the organization as well as *against*. This distinction will be elaborated on in the next section; given the amounts, we have classified these as fraud against the organization.)

The KPMG data, with the aforementioned additional categories superimposed, provide the profile in Exhibit E.1.

The relative frequencies of KPMG's reported false financial-statement fraud (5 percent), bribery and corruption (15 percent), and asset misappropriations (80 percent) are exactly in line with the frequencies for those categories reported in the ACFE 1996 "Report to the Nation."

KPMG 1998 Survey			Type of Fraud		
			"Against" the Organization	"For" the Organization	
Fraud Classification	Average Loss	Number of Organizations		False Financial Statements	Bribery and Corruption
False Financial Statements	$1,239,000	12		X	
Bribery and Corruption:					
Bid Rigging/ Price-Fixing	$342,000	8			X
Conflict of Interest	$38,000	10	X		
Kickbacks	$35,000	10	X		
Subtotal		37			
Misappropriation:					
Inventory Theft	$346,000	43	X		
False Invoices/ Phantom Vendors	$256,000	49	X		
Diversion of Sales	$180,000	6	X		
Expense Accounts	$141,000	44	X		
Unnecessary and Personal Use Purchasing	$63,000	40	X		
Payroll Fraud	$26,000	9	X		
Subtotal		191			
Total		240			

EXHIBIT E.1   KPMG Survey Data

Classification: Management Fraud Categories

W e used the categories of the ACFE 1996 "Report to the Nation" as a starting point in developing our classifications of management fraud, to provide a frame of reference to ensure we didn't omit any significant major category.

The categories that we eventually considered primarily management fraud can be depicted as shown in Exhibit F.1.

The starting-point comparison between our categories and the ACFE's can also be illustrated by the mapping to the categories of Occupational Fraud and Abuse shown in Exhibit F.2. Those categories we consider pri-

AGAINST Misappropriation	FOR Financial Reporting
Vendor Billing Schemes (Shell Companies) Other Disbursements Inventory Certain Diverted Receipts Schemes (Normally Employee Fraud)	Fraudulent Financial Reporting
	Corruption
Corruption	Illegal Acts (e.g., money laundering) Commercial Bribery Price-Fixing/Bid Rigging International Arena
Conflict of Interst Bribery (Bid Rigging)	

EXHIBIT F.1   Categories of Major Management Fraud

	Occupational Fraud and Abuse	Our Management Fraud Categories For/Against the Organization	
	Median Loss	Against	For
(Bold = Management Fraud)			
Fraudulent Reporting:			
Financial statements	$5,000,000*		X
Non-financial statements	3,050,000*		X
(financial statements)			
Corruption:			
Bribery	$500,000	X	
Conflict of interest	500,000	X	
Economic extortion (bribery)	167,000	X	
Illegal gratuities	8,107		
Misappropriation:			
Vendor billing	250,000	X	
Other fraudulent			
disbursements	140,000	X	
Inventory and assets	100,000	X	
Check tampering	96,432		
Skimming	50,000	X	
Payroll	50,000		
Check register	22,500		
Cash larceny	22,000		
Expense reports	20,000		
Other	107,230		

*Amount of misstatement rather than actual loss.

EXHIBIT F.2   ACFE Survey Data and Management Fraud

marily management fraud are indicated in **bold,** with their classifications as for or against the organization.

As you can see by the median losses shown in Exhibit F.2, our categories of management fraud represent a considerable majority of the total loss from occupational fraud. Check tampering, payroll fraud, check register fraud, cash larceny, and expense reports are employee-type fraud: The essential nature of this type of fraud is nonmanagerial—that is, it is not based on positional authority nor is it relationship-based and it appears on the books. The lower median losses for these classifications support this categorization.

We have classified fraudulent reporting as being for the organization, because it certainly is not against the organization. In so doing, we recognized the need for a new dimension: A considerable amount of management fraud, at least initially, is ostensibly for the organization.

Thus we added fraud for the organization to our classification scheme. Although it involves potential negative consequences for the organization, the more important aspect for us is that fraud *for* the organization frequently begets fraud *against* the organization.

Consequently, in addition to the categories of occupational fraud and abuse, our classification system includes the following as fraud *for* the organization:

- Illegal acts (e.g., money laundering)
- Commercial bribery
- Price-fixing/bid rigging
- Fraud in the international arena (black sales and bribery)

Glossary of Terms

Rather than defining these terms in the broader context of their common usage, my focus is on their limited meaning and usage within this book, with apologies to Webster.

ACL—This stands for "Audit Command Language," and is a particularly useful software for interactive, iterative analyses of large data files and/or other CAATs. See also **CAATs.**

Anomaly in System for Performance Accountability—A fancy way of describing the cubbyholes in the structure for recorded accountability that permit hiding fraudulent debits or diverting transactions to keep them off the books. Put simply, this supplies the opportunity to keep the effect of the fraud off the P&L.

Asset Misappropriation—The most common of the three major categories of occupational fraud defined by the ACFE "Reports to the Nation." As the term implies, this type of fraud involves conversion of organizational assets via deception. In the 1996 report, 80 percent of all fraud was asset misappropriation; in the 2002 report, approximately 86 percent was. Most of this type of fraud is committed by employees, is on the books, and involves taking advantage of internal control weaknesses. As such, the typical loss is smaller than that for the other major categories: The median loss from each instance of corruption ($530,000) was 6.6 times that from asset misappropriation ($80,000) in the 2002 "Report to the Nation."

Benford's Law—Developed by Frank Benford, this concerns expected distributions of digits in normally occurring data. By comparing the actual frequencies to the expected frequencies, the presence of artificially created data can be highlighted for follow-up.

Bid Rigging—The circumvention of controls intended to be provided by competitive bidding. This circumvention can occur in numerous ways: on the front end (i.e., by release of confidential information to one or more bidders, or by unbalanced bidding), during the administration of the contract (by change orders), or by collusion among the bidders (in which case it would be fraud for their respective organizations).

Black Sales—In the international arena, this term refers to unrecorded sales that are usually made by cash to circumvent tax regulations. These types of transactions are fairly common in many Latin American countries and lesser-developed countries.

Bribery—A quid-pro-quo arrangement whereby something of value is offered to influence an official act. Traditionally, the act would be a decision by a governmental agent or employee acting in official capacity. The term *commercial bribery* broadens the traditional definition to include business as well as governmental transactions. See also **Kickbacks.**

CAATs—This acronym stands for "computer-assisted audit techniques." Many perceptive observers believe CAATs are the wave of the future.

Channel Stuffing—A form of revenue-recognition fraud accomplished by various methods of bill-and-hold—that is, shipping products for which a sale actually has not yet occurred.

Commercial Bribery—See **Bribery.**

Conflict of Interest—A subset of corruption (against the organization). Basically, a relationship or arrangement which is not in the best interest of the organization. Given the managerial positional leverage, such conflict-of-interest managerial fraud represents the largest area of loss for the typical organization (see **Sweet Spot of Management Fraud**). While this type of fraud can occur on the books, the larger, more complex instances are frequently off the books.

Continuous Monitoring—Ongoing examination of data or systems in accordance with predetermined criteria or programs. In particular, in the context of this book, this involves typically information-technology-driven real-time data analysis of the organization's books, records, and related information designed to identify anomalies for follow-up.

Corruption—From *Black's Law Dictionary:* "The act of an official or *fiduciary* person who *unlawfully and wrongfully uses his* [*position*] to [obtain] some *benefit for himself* or another . . . *contrary to duty and the rights of others*" [emphasis ours]. While the definition is somewhat archaic, the notion of abrogating fiduciary duty by using one's position contrary to duty fits this type of management fraud perfectly.

   Corruption is one of the three major categories of occupational fraud defined by the ACFE "Reports to the Nation." In the 1996 report, 15 percent of all cases of fraud fell into this category; in the 2002 report, approximately 13 percent did. Most of these cases of fraud are committed by management, are off the books, and involve override rather than internal control weaknesses. In the 2002 report, the median loss from each instance of corruption ($530,000) was 6.6 times that from asset misappropriation ($80,000).[1]

Criminogenic Industries—Industries in which the traditional and/or expected norm of behavior is fraudulent ("It's a way of life"). Typically, this is considered fraud *for* the company.

Detection—The second step in the recognition, detection, and investigation fraud chain. The line between recognition and detection is frequently blurred. The author contends that all internal auditors should have the capability of recognizing the symptoms of fraud, and all experienced auditors should be able to develop that recognition into an evaluation of the need for additional investigation. However, "[t]he internal auditor . . . is not expected to have the expertise of a person whose primary responsibility is detecting and investigating fraud."[2] See also **Investigation, Recognition,** and **Responsibility for Fraud Detection.**

Discretionary Reserves—Reserves that involve a high degree of *subjective* estimates, and are consequently more susceptible to management manipulation.

Employee Fraud—As distinct from management fraud, employee fraud is the most common, constituting 58 percent of all occupational fraud,[3] and typically involves asset misappropriation, usually involves internal control weaknesses, and results in the lowest level of loss. The median loss from each instance of management non-financial-statement fraud is five times higher than that from employee-committed fraud.

Financial-Reporting Fraud—This is the least common of the three major occupational fraud categories of the ACFE "Reports to the Nation." In both reports, 5 percent of all cases of fraud involved fraudulent financial statements.[4] Most of these were committed by senior management—the COSO report on fraudulent financial reporting indicated that 83 percent of these cases of fraud involved the CEO and/or CFO[5]—and actually involve override of internal controls.

Foreign Corrupt Practices Act—The Foreign Corrupt Practices Act (FCPA) of 1977 was designed to eliminate bribes by U.S. companies to foreign governmental officials. In addition to the antibribery provisions, the more pervasive effect has been the bookkeeping requirements.

Fraud—"Fraud encompasses an array of irregularities and illegal acts characterized by *intentional deception*"[6] [emphasis ours].

Investigation—The last step in the recognition, detection, and investigation fraud chain. Investigation is a more specialized, frequently quasi- or paralegal process. "The internal auditor . . . is not expected to have the expertise of a person whose primary responsibility is detecting and investigating fraud."[7] This book provides sufficient guidance for experienced internal auditors to hold up their end while working as part of an investigative team with representatives from the security and law functions. See also **Detection, Recognition,** and **Responsibility for Fraud Detection.**

Kickbacks—Bribes, usually expressed as payment of a percentage of ill-gotten gains, designed to influence an act contrary to the fiduciary duty of the individual being influenced. Normally, the payment occurs after, or as, the ill-gotten gains are realized. (A bribe is commonly thought of as a fixed-sum amount and is normally paid in advance.)

Legalistic Workaround—An unbalanced emphasis on the end justifying the means whereby convoluted structures and/or processes are devised to accomplish business objectives of questionable legality—for example, circumvention of the bribery provisions of the Foreign Corrupt Practices Act. See also **Overriding Objective.**

Middleman—Recognizably artificial positioning between the expected normal suppliers or customers and the company. "Middleman" is a subset of the broader term "related party." The ongoing nature of a stream of commercial transactions distinguishes a middleman relationship from a related-party situation.

Money Laundering—The movement of funds whereby proceeds derived from illegal activities are exchanged into usable, seemingly legitimate funds. As this relates to the normal internal audit concern, note that organizations are typically not the source of the illicit funds that are being laundered; rather, they are used to provide the means by which the funds are laundered, or they might be "looking the other way" while accepting clearly questionable funds.

Occupational Fraud—This is simply fraud committed by an executive, a manager, an employee, or, in the broadest sense, an agent in the conduct of their employment. This stands in obvious contrast to external fraud against the organization.

Operating-Management Fraud—The 1996 ACFE "Report to the Nation" says 30 percent of all cases of fraud are committed by managers (as distinct from executives/owners). The author believes that a considerable majority of fraudulent cases of corruption against the organization (largely conflict of interest) are committed by this stratum (i.e., the level below senior management), and further, that this is the largest single area of loss from occupational fraud. See also **Sweet Spot of Management Fraud.**

Overriding Objective—An undue top-down organizational emphasis on only one dimension, but not necessarily on "making the numbers." Rather, this overemphasis may open the door to uneconomical practices with unintended consequences, such as various types of conflict-of-interest schemes. See also **Legalistic Workaround.**

Prevention—The various means, such as a code of ethics or company hot line, that an organization uses to prevent fraud. The author believes that the probability of detection and prosecution is ultimately the only effective form of prevention. See also **Risk/Reward Dynamic.**

Price-Fixing—Price-fixing for the organization is the circumvention of competitive market forces. The classic form is dividing market shares and/or coordinating prices among companies that should be competitive.

Recognition—The first step in the recognition, detection, and investigation fraud chain. This is the most important fraud-related function of the internal auditor: "Internal auditors should have sufficient knowledge of fraud to identify the indicators that fraud may have been committed, [and] be alert to opportunities that could allow fraud."[8] See also **Detection, Investigation,** and **Responsibility for Fraud Detection.**

Related Party(ies)—"Middleman" is a subset of the broader term "related party." In common usage, this term usually refers to the lack of arms-length dealing, and typically relates to valuation issues and/or conflict of interest. The FASB provides a limited definition of "related party" as "a member of management," which would include directors, top officers, vice presidents in charge of major business units, and "other persons who perform similar policymaking functions."

Responsibility for Fraud Detection—"Internal auditors should have sufficient knowledge of fraud to identify the indicators that fraud may have been committed, be alert to opportunities that could allow fraud, evaluate the need for additional investigation, and notify the appropriate authorities. The internal auditor . . . is not expected to have the expertise of a person whose primary responsibility is detecting and investigating fraud."[9] See also **Detection, Investigation,** and **Recognition.**

Risk/Reward Dynamic—The aspiring perpetrator of fraud weighs the risk of detection and prosecution against the rewards of the fraud. The author contends that the risks have diminished at the same time that the rewards have risen, thereby skewing this dynamic.

Senior Management Fraud—The 1996 ACFE "Report to the Nation" contends that 12 percent of all occupational fraud is committed by executives or owners, the majority of which would presumably fall into this category. A considerable majority of cases involving fraudulent financial statements are committed at the direction of senior management, and are the most representative type of fraud for this stratum.

Shell Company—A variation of disbursement fraud involving a fictitious company and payment for nonexistent goods or services. Shell companies are also known as *phantom vendors.*

Swaps or Reciprocal Sales—Tactics used to overstate revenue, primarily to create the impression of growth near the end of the stock market bubble. The classic examples occurred in telecommunications and in certain energy companies whereby simultaneous purchases and sales of essentially the same asset at the same price furthered the illusion of growth.

Sweet Spot of Management Fraud—See **Conflict of Interest.** A considerable majority of the million-dollar cases of fraud against organizations are managerial fraud. Moreover, given the much higher average loss from bribery and corruption, a majority of these cases of million-dollar fraud fall into that category. Thus, it is reasonable to conclude that the largest single area of loss is managerial corruption against the company. We frequently refer to this as the "sweet spot."

Telltale Debit(s)—If you are going to commit fraud on the books, you have to hide the otherwise telltale debit.

Notes

CHAPTER 1

1. Institute of Internal Auditors (IIA), former standard 280-04.
2. Association of Certified Fraud Examiners (ACFE), "Report to the Nation on Occupational Fraud and Abuse," 2002.
3. Ibid.
4. IIA, Standard 1210.A2, Standards for the Professional Practice of Internal Auditing.
5. IIA, Practice Advisory 1210.A2-1: Identification of Fraud.
6. ACFE, "Report to the Nation on Occupational Fraud and Abuse," 1996 and 2002.

CHAPTER 2

1. Joseph T. Wells, *Occupational Fraud and Abuse* (Austin, TX: Obsidian Publishing Company, 1997).
2. ACFE, 1996 report.
3. ACFE, 2002 report.
4. Wells, *Occupational Fraud and Abuse.*
5. ACFE, 1996 report.
6. ACFE, 2002 report.
7. ACFE, 1996 report.
8. ACFE, 2002 report.
9. Ibid.
10. KPMG, 1998 Fraud Survey, 1999.
11. Ibid.
12. ACFE, 1996 report.
13. ACFE, 1996 and 2002 reports.
14. Ibid.
15. Wells, *Occupational Fraud and Abuse.*
16. ACFE, 1996 report.

CHAPTER 3

1. ACFE, 1996 report.

CHAPTER 4

1. KPMG, 1998 survey.

CHAPTER 6

1. KPMG, 1998 survey.
2. ACFE, 1996 report.
3. Wells, *Occupational Fraud and Abuse.*
4. Treadway Commission, Committee of Sponsoring Organizations (COSO), "Fraudulent Financial Reporting: 1987–1997—An Analysis of U.S. Public Companies," 1999 (www.coso.org).
5. KPMG, 1998 survey.
6. Ibid.
7. ACFE, 1996 report.

CHAPTER 7

1. COSO, "Fraudulent Financial Reporting: 1987–1997."
2. *U.S. News & World Report,* June 24, 2002.
3. Baruch Lev, "Manager's Journal," *The Wall Street Journal,* January 28, 2003.
4. Transparency International, Bribe Payers Index, 2002 (www.Transparency.org).
5. Ibid.
6. Seymour Hersh, "The Price of Oil," *The New Yorker,* July 9, 2001.
7. Stephen Rosoff, Henry Pontell, and Robert Tillman, *Profit without Honor: White-Collar Crime and the Looting of America,* 2nd ed. (Upper Saddle River, N.J.: Prentice Hall, 2002).
8. Ibid., p. 65.
9. Ibid., p. 73.
10. ACFE, 1996 report.
11. Wells, *Occupational Fraud and Abuse.*
12. Transparency International, Bribe Payers Index.

CHAPTER 8

1. IIA, Practice Advisory 1210.A2-1. Identification of Fraud.

CHAPTER 9

1. David Coderre, *Fraud Detection: Using Data Analysis Techniques to Detect Fraud* (Vancouver, B.C.: Global Audit Publications, 1999).
2. Ibid.
3. Mark Nigrini, *Digital Analysis Using Benford's Law* (Vancouver, B.C.: Global Audit Publications, 2000).

CHAPTER 10

1. ACFE, 2002 report.
2. IIA, Practice Advisory 1210.A2-1: Identification of Fraud.
3. Donald Cressey, *Other People's Money* (Montclair, N.J.: Patterson Smith, 1973).

APPENDIX D

1. COSO, "Fraudulent Financial Reporting: 1987–1997."

APPENDIX E

1. Literally, as this book was going to press, on December 1, 2003, KPMG Forensic announced the completion of Fraud Survey 2003 on CNBC. Based on interviews with 450 executives, KPMG reports "organizations are reporting a rise in fraud, responding with expanded fraud measures . . . and planning future actions . . ." See *www.us.kpmg.com/news/index* for the survey.

GLOSSARY OF TERMS

1. ACFE, 1996 and 2002 reports.
2. IIA, Practice Advisory 1210.A2-2; related standard: 1210.A2.
3. ACFE, 1996 and 2002 reports.
4. Ibid.
5. COSO, "Fraudulent Financial Reporting: 1987–1997."
6. IIA, former standard 280-04.
7. IIA, Standard 1210.A2.
8. IIA, Practice Advisory 1210.A2-2.
9. Ibid.; related standards 1210.A2.

Index